RIVER ROCKS

CONTEMPORARY APPLICATION
OF ETERNAL PRINCIPLES

H. Maurice Lednicky

Blessings!

H. Maurice Lednicky

ISBN: 978-0-7361-0617-7

Publishing assistance provided by:

Life Publishers International
1625 North Robberson Avenue
Springfield, Missouri 65803
United States of America
417.831.7766

TABLE OF CONTENTS

iii

RIVER ROCKS

CONTEMPORARY APPLICATION OF ETERNAL PRINCIPLES

The life of Joshua is quite intriguing. He must have been an extraordinary young man. He was one of the twelve spies that Moses sent into Canaan. And, one of two who came back with a positive report and urged immediate action. By the way, only those two spies–Joshua and Caleb–entered the Promised Land. Remember, all the adults who were twenty years old or older when they were delivered from Egyptian captivity died in the wilderness wanderings for their lack of faith. Strangely, they had faith to leave Egypt and cross the Red Sea, but not sufficient faith to cross the Jordan River and enter into this covenant land.

Joshua was Moses' "minister" (Exodus 24:13; 33:11) and chosen by the Lord (Numbers 27:15-20) as successor to the only leader Israel have ever known since their miraculous departure from Egyptian captivity. But, now, Moses is dead. This new leader has the formidable task of leading this younger generation into the Land of Promise. That day finally arrives and it is time to cross the Jordan River, which is swollen out of its banks. The inspired record (Joshua 4) is a faith-building story. This generation walked across Jordan on dry land–just as their parents had done at the Red Sea. It was a miracle of the magnitude that had only been repeated to them. Perhaps as they grew up these youngsters grew weary with hearing it repeated over and over again. Or, maybe, the miraculous event had gradually faded from their parents' minds as the years dragged on and the sameness of life took its toll on them. Before this particular day, this generation had never witnessed anything so astounding. There are many explicit examples and powerful truths in God's progressive revelation of Himself to His children. And, they should not soon be forgotten.

That is the point here. Did you notice that Joshua commanded that twelve stones (one for each of the twelve tribes of Israel) be stacked in the *"middle of the Jordan"* (Joshua 4:9) at the very place the priests who carried the Ark of the Covenant were standing? And, another twelve stones from that same location were taken to the other side of the River (inside Canaan) to be a *"memorial among the people of Israel forever"* (Joshua 4:7). Very significant. One stack of stones marked the spot identifying the very visible presence of God (Ark of the Covenant) and the other was a testimony of God's glorious intervention. But, these memorials were not just for that moment or that specific group of people. Joshua provides insight into the far reaching intention of piling these river rocks at this location. *"In the future your children will ask you, 'What do these stones mean?' Then you can tell them, 'They remind us that the Jordan River stopped flowing when the Ark of the Lord's Covenant went across'"* (Joshua 4:6-7 NLT). The presence and the power of God were here. Remembered by twenty-four rocks. There is no scriptural evidence that the stones were all the same size or shape or color. Nothing says that the Israelites designed them in a special or specific way before stacking the stones. But, regardless of the simplicity, they represented the place where God had revealed Himself in a supernatural manner. The revelation of the Almighty–His nature, His attributes, His redemptive plan must always be at the forefront of our thinking and lodged deep within our spirit.

That is the message of this compilation of writings. The truths of God's Word are unchanging. Cultures, geography, and generations never alter divine principles. *"God is not a man, that He should lie"* (Numbers 23:19, KJV). *"By no means! Let God be found true though every human being is false and a liar, as it is written, That You may be justified and shown to be upright in what You say, and prevail when You are judged [by sinful men]'"* (Romans 3:4, AMP) (See Psalm 51:4). So, with that single axiomatic priority, it is unequivocally correct to declare that His Word is absolute truth. This we must believe. It is imperative to have a non-negotiable faith grip on the one true God. It is foundational to all that follows in our teaching/preaching. As in the analogy mentioned, the truth is the truth, even if cultural or generational customs and mores may be constantly shifting.

If biblical record and human history provide any empirical evidence of humanity's repeated rejection of eternal truth, then a strong word of caution is in order. Constantly monitoring our spirit and mind lest any seed of doubt be planted should be a regular routine in light of the expansion of sin and evil in this culture. The divine plan and process have never deviated one Planck length (equivalent to a millionth of a billionth of a billionth of a billionth of a centimeter) or one attosecond (equivalent to one quintillionth of a second). They are the eternally unchanging!

Our Creator God is infinitely wise and did not attempt to provide information into His ways and redemptive plan that coincided with the ideologies and practices of specific cultures or subcultures, language groups, or political persuasions. Divine foreknowledge allows Him to see the exponential expansion of evil that has been developing from generation to generation. Consequently, He gave us truth in the form of principles rather than trying to put a specific title to every new expression of disobedience. In this sense, while the truth is unchanging, the approach to revealing the mutation of sinful behavior is very different. To be certain, since Adam and Eve broke the personal relationship, and thus the fellowship, with the Father in Eden, all humankind has a depraved nature—a bent toward evil. *"For all have sinned, and come short of the glory of God"* (Romans 3:23, KJV). In a practical application, there are new, more egregious and perverted expressions of outright disdain for the commands of the Lord today. Just one example is same-sex marriage. One of the earliest instructions of the Lord to man and woman was to *"be fruitful and multiply"* (Genesis 1:28, KJV). It is foolish to even have to say that two men or two women cannot bear children. It simply is not possible. In my personal evaluation, this is one of Satan's last attempts to destroy humankind and subsequently defeat the redemptive plan of God.

Bible scholars have long since loudly proclaimed the significance of the marriage between hermeneutics (proper interpretation of Scripture) and homiletics (proper application of Scripture). Proper interpretation requires knowing the "backstory" (context) of the passage. It precludes the popular practice of invoking selective verses for establishing a biblical doctrine/truth. Theological integrity and honesty are twin tracks that must never be relinquished in favor of contemporary human-centered (cultural, geographical, and/or religious) explanations of the Word of God.

Now, for the different aspect. The Gospels provide powerful insights into the appropriate application (homiletics) of scriptural principles. Jesus told stories (parables) to the crowds who followed Him and heard His teaching. In that era/location/culture the primary means of livelihood was agriculture (farming, livestock, fishing, etc.). To communicate truth with the vast audiences that followed Him, our Lord spoke of the natural things to illustrate spiritual principles. Then, when in discussion with His closest followers, His explanation took on a much deeper dimension of the eternal principles. Going beyond the New Testament era, the technological, medical, educational, and lifestyle changes have been exponential. If nothing else came into play, the illustrative comparisons of past years would be lost on this generation. The opposite is also true. Can you imagine a rural farmer of the 1800s comprehending social media, sermon illustrations about cell phones or a video clip in the middle of a sermon? The point is that the Word must be primary, using illustrative material with the intent of clarifying the Truth, not the other way around.

This collection of various missives relates to matters of spiritual truth that have (1) been neglected, (2) been misunderstood, (3) been misrepresented, (4) fallen victim to cultural standards, or (5) even (worse), become an integral part of preaching/teaching that is in direct contradiction with the God-given principles of Scripture. Understand that I am viewing this through my experiential grid, which, by the Father's grace, has afforded me opportunities to stand on all four corners of ministry/life intersections. In the pressure of personal reality, it is possible for our perspective to become myopic. That is natural since, as believers, we sincerely want to understand God and present Him as a just, loving heavenly Father. But even with the purest of motives, trying to explain/defend the ways of the Sovereign Almighty can lead us along a path that comes up short of answers. The devil uses these moments to taunt us with doubt (is God able?) and fear (is God willing?).

This booklet in no way seeks to be all-inclusive. You probably have this many or more subjects that play in your mind. The ONE overriding truth that is foundational to the stability/maturity of our faith is TRUST. He alone is worthy of our total confidence. Our God has the eternal record as evidence of His faithfulness to honor/fulfill His Word from before earthly creation until this very moment. He has never failed—and He never will!

WHY IS THIS HAPPENING?

Good question! There are at least three possibilities. Let me note them and then attempt to offer a brief scriptural basis for these conclusions and weave them together with the goodness of a loving heavenly Father.

1. **The natural course of life.** Age happens (experience is speaking here). Machines wear out/break. Frustrations occur at home/on the job. Every flat tire is not a satanic attack—it could be the lack of financial resource or even negligence. It is simply living in this present world that remains "under the curse." It is significant that Adam was to work in (cultivate, tend, work, take care of, Genesis 2:15) the Garden of Eden before he sinned. However, the consequence of disobedience included painful childbearing for women, difficulty in providing food from a harsh earth, and, of course, physical death (3:16–19). By the way, Adam and Eve broke fellowship with a holy God at the moment they sinned. In many instances these unpleasant events that seem to be unrelenting and ever present are not an "attack of the enemy," nor can they be described as "discipline" (training) from the Lord. They are the daily ups and downs of life.

2. **A direct attack from Satan.** The devil is hard pressed to relinquish any space that he occupies/controls (which is much of this world). So to stop a believer from functioning as a light to reveal his darkness, he attacks. During the

earthly life of Jesus, He, the perfect Son of God, was frequently attacked by Satan. The most commonly known is the temptation in the wilderness that followed His baptism by John the Baptist (Matthew 3:13–4:11). By the way, I personally believe that Jesus fully understood His mission to earth at this moment. Baptism symbolizes death, burial, and resurrection. The evil one even offered Christ an escape from death on the cross (vv.4:8–11). But this was not the only attack of Satan against Christ. When the crisis moment arrived, as a man Jesus struggled with the suffering, pain, and death that was inevitable. His final prayer before the crucifixion was, "*If it is possible, let this cup of suffering* (death) *be taken away from me. Yet I want your will to be done, not mine*" (Matthew 26:39, NLT, emphasis, addition mine). To dull the influence of the Lord's Church, Satan deceives and brings confusion within the Body of Christ.

3. A spiritual lesson from the Lord. The writer of Hebrews calls this "*discipline,*" but it must be carefully distinguished from *punishment* for disobedience. In times that challenge our spiritual maturity, and perhaps even our faith, the Holy Spirit shines the spotlight of reality into the most sheltered/hidden crevices of our heart. Here we often discover what we did not even know or realize and, more than likely, would not have believed was locked in some dark closet of our spirit. Watchman Nee, the well-known Chinese church leader and teacher during the first half of the twentieth century, brought this truth very close to home in his writings. His famous quote "God's basic work is to reduce us"[1] still resonates with the humble servant of the Lord who desires to walk in fellowship with the Father. In his letter to the Philippian believers, Paul declares his willingness to "*suffer with him* (Christ), *sharing in his death, so that one way or another I will experience the resurrection from the dead!*" (Philippians 3:10–11, NLT, addition mine). A loving Father wants us to see ourselves and learn how He can change us for our benefit and His glory.

Assuming that we accept these observations, then it is also realistic to acknowledge that we cannot always easily discern which of the three possibilities is in play for any specific event. But one thing is certain: no matter the circumstance, its origination, or the ultimate outcome, if we are willing and obedient, God will use it as a means of spiritual growth/maturation that will honor His name. *"And we know that all things work together for good to them that love God, to them who are the called according to his purpose"* (Romans 8:28, KJV).

Now, a moment to evaluate the previously mentioned factors impacting this temporary/earthly pilgrimage:

1. The ultimate consequence of disobedience (sin in the Garden of Eden) is death. From the first man/woman (Adam/Eve), natural (physical) death normally comes as a process. (Lest we forget, Adam and Eve died spiritually on the very day they disobeyed the single prohibition God had given. God had not been untruthful, as the serpent had tried to convince them.) But sooner or later, death comes to everyone—no exceptions (Hebrews 9:27; Romans 5:12; etc.). Two scriptural truths: (1) man is depraved (Isaiah 53:6; Romans 3:23), and (2) the entire world is negatively impacted by the resultant actions (Romans 8:18–23). So, weaving our way through this present mixture of valleys, plains, and mountains, we are on a one-way journey toward eternity. And that simply means we are

> God's grace is for living as surely as it is for dying!

not exempt from daily frustrations/struggles that often "rain on our parade." Repeat it over and over. Settle it deep in your mind and heart: if we allow Him to do so, God will receive glory from even the rather routine/mundane course of daily living. And resultantly, His glory always accrues to our spiritual benefit.

2. The enemy of God is inferior (not an opposite equal) to the Almighty, but not to man. Literally, in our own abilities, strength, or goodness, we are no match for Satan. But he is a liar and the father of lies—Jesus said so (John 8:44)! He is a deceiver and comes disguised as *"an angel of light"* (2 Corinthians 11:14). Paul admonishes believers to be alert as *"we are not unaware of his schemes"* (2 Corinthians 2:11, NIV). Empowered by the Spirit and armed with the Word of God, we are wise and stand courageously, firmly, and confidently (Ephesians 6:10–17). This in no way implies that we are not involved in every aspect of spiritual war. Many battles are fierce, but we are victors, not spiritual casualties (1 John 4:4; Revelation 12:11). Paul excitedly declares, *"No, despite all these things, <u>overwhelming victory</u> is ours through Christ, who loved us"* (Romans 8:37, NLT, emphasis mine).

3. **Knowing/accepting that the *"thorn in the flesh"* (2 Corinthians 12:7–10) is for our spiritual benefit is always a challenge.** It was to Paul. He earnestly prayed for deliverance. Finally, the Lord told him to stop asking—it was not going to happen. (By the way, two of the biblical giants, Moses and Paul, are the only two who were ever instructed to stop praying!) At that dramatic point Paul understood that its purpose was to keep him from pride. Success at any level is difficult to keep in perspective. A good Father is constantly monitoring our behavior and heart attitudes. He knows when we need to be brought back into line.

The illustration the writer of Hebrews employs is a comparison between the discipline of an earthly father and the discipline of the heavenly Father (Hebrews 12:5–11). My parents were strong disciplinarians. You know the type—they made me study in school, eat my food, work, go to church, be polite to adults, and punished me for disobedience. It wasn't always the most enjoyable. Often I did not understand their logic. Never did I believe the mantra "This hurts me worse than it hurts you"—until I became a father. However, now I am extremely grateful for such training! Today we call it "tough love." The Father does not want His children to self-destruct!

Well, these comments probably lead us to conclude that definitive answers are not always simple—or perhaps even possible for our restricted access to the unseen/unknown. It may be best if we do not search so diligently to ascertain the origin of any circumstance/difficulty. The takeaway for me:

1. God is a good, loving heavenly Father.

2. He is *never* taken by surprise by any of the small or major events that often catch us off guard. Let's stamp it in the forefront of our minds: God knows the beginning from the end, along with all the valleys and mountains, streams and oceans, forests and pastures we must go over, through, or around on our journey home.

3. He is greater than any force of hell or any person being used by the "accuser of the brethren" to harm His children or Christ's Church.

4. He is sovereign—His way is not only best; it is perfect. *"As for God, his way is perfect: the word of the Lord is flawless; he as a shield for all who take refuge in him"* (Psalm 18:30, NIV; 2 Samuel 22:31, NIV).

5. If I trust Him with every aspect of my life, He will be pleased and ultimately lead me to victory, joy, and peace by His grace!

Endnotes
1 Watchman Nee, *The Glorious Church, 2nd ed.* (Anaheim, CA: Living Stream Ministry, 1993), 133.

MY THOUGHTS:

STUMBLING TOWARD PERFECTION

The proverbs of Solomon are a source of constant wisdom. In fact, *"their purpose is to teach people wisdom and discipline, to help them understand the insights of the wise...Let the wise listen to these proverbs and become even wiser"* (Proverbs 1:2, 5, NLT).

So, in my personal Bible reading, I turn often to this book and ask the Holy Spirit to illuminate these truths to my mind/ heart. This verse captured my attention recently:

> *"The godly may trip seven times, but they will get up again"* (Proverbs 24:16, NLT).

> *"For a just man falleth seven times, and riseth up again"* (KJV).

A foundational biblical understanding of a personal encounter with Christ (revelation, repentance, restoration) assures the petitioner that the result is justification.

> *"Therefore , since we have been <u>justified</u> by faith, we have <u>peace with God</u> through our Lord Jesus Christ, through whom we also have access by faith into this <u>grace</u> in which we stand, and so we rejoice in <u>hope of the glory</u> of God"* (Romans 5:1–2, MEV, emphasis mine; also see Galatians 3:24; Titus 3:7).

Justification is the formal acquittal of sin. Or, as one theologian said, "Just-as-if it had never been there."

Positionally, before the heavenly Father at that very moment, I am without guilt or condemnation.

> *"Therefore, if any man is in Christ, he is a new creature. Old things have passed away. Look, all things have become new"* (2 Corinthians 5:17, MEV; also see Romans 8:1–2).

But now comes the challenge. How do I actualize that spiritual experience in daily living? Growing, developing, maturing in the faith walk is an important scriptural truth.

> *"But grow in the <u>grace</u> and <u>knowledge</u> of our Lord and Savior Jesus Christ. <u>To Him be glory</u>, both now and forever. Amen"* (2 Peter 3:18, MEV, emphasis mine; also see Ephesians 4:11–16).

Absolute perfection in this earthly life? No one of us can ever achieve such a noble goal. The Adamic nature constantly haunts us. This brief moment in our eternal history is probationary. It is, as it were, "basic training" that frequently requires strenuous tests and strict discipline (Hebrews 12:1–4).

By definition the words *fall* and *trip* imply two specific things:

1. To be knocked down or tripped by some outside intervention (i.e., the devil or someone acting on his behalf)

2. To come short of the desired goal (i.e., yield to the pressure of evil temptation)

Honest evaluation requires an admission that at some point in our walk of faith, we all know the reality of being less than spiritually mature. Perhaps we were disciplined enough to control our external behavior; perhaps not. If our choices are flawed, it inevitably has a negative impact on the desired spiritual progress. Of even greater challenge in our pursuit toward godly growth and development is what occupies our thought patterns.

> *"For out of the abundance of the heart* (thoughts/attitudes/motives) *the mouth speaks. A good man out of the good treasure of his heart brings forth good things. And an evil man out of the evil treasure brings forth evil things"* (Jesus in Matthew 12:34–35, MEV, explanations mine).

Motives (hidden, inner thoughts) were significant in the ministry of Jesus. For example, the major thrust of the Sermon on the Mount (Matthew 5–7) was about motivation. Jesus did not condemn good works or obedience to the law of Moses. What was penetrating to those who professed to be spiritual leaders was His divine insight into what was in their heart of hearts. While motivation guides the thought process, it can often be secretly maintained internally, with little expression given externally. Perhaps the private part of us demands stricter discipline and constant monitoring to prevent stymied progress toward greater spiritual maturity.

But the wisdom from Solomon is that a righteous person will not give up when he/she stumbles and stumbles and stumbles—even seven times!

- No turning around because the faith walk is too difficult
- No assuming that following Christ is no longer worth the effort
- No wallowing in self-pity
- No stopping to justify bad personal choices/behavior
- No finger-pointing at others to distract from self
- No lashing out angrily and vowing to get revenge

- No accusations against the Almighty

The righteous will get up and keep moving toward the eternal goal.

Stumbling? Yes! Abandon the spiritual race? Never.

So if you have been knocked down, have tripped up, or feel like a total failure—don't quit.

The hand of the Lord is reaching for you.

His plan is to empower you with grace and strength.

Get up. Keep moving forward.

You do not have to repeatedly make the same mistakes.

There is a glorious throng of heavenly witnesses who completed the journey (Hebrews 12:1–2). It can be done!

They stumbled...

    but kept getting up...

        all the way to glorious perfection!

MY THOUGHTS:

"NEVER TRAINED FOR DEFEAT"

Last evening we were watching a TV special (celebrating Veterans Day) featuring several veterans who had served in various war zones over the past decade or two. It was very informative to hear their assessment of what they had encountered in the life-death struggles for survival. It was also quite inspiring to hear of their unrestrained commitment to the mission and their loyalty to each other as a unit.

To be perfectly clear, this is not a defense of war, nor a statement as to the political correctness of one nation in combat with another nation. There are various opinions on this subject, and this article is being used only as an illustration of the victory promised to God's children in the battles of our earthly journey.

By the way, the inspired Scriptures employ many military terms as analogies in defining/describing the believer's walk of faith. For example, "soldiers" (2 Timothy 2:3–4), "armor of God" (Ephesians 6:11, 13), "weapons of warfare are not carnal" (2 Corinthians 10:4, KJV), "fight the good fight of faith" (1 Timothy 6:12; 2 Timothy 4:7), etc. Obviously, such terminology in this biblical context does not refer to actual physical weapons or wars among nations.

Back to the TV program. It was quite interesting that these military men, who had been in the worst of the worst situations, spoke frequently of their "men" as family, the loyalty they had for each member of the unit, and the singularity of purpose in accomplishing that specific mission. As I listened, it seemed that the military had adopted numerous scriptural principles that define the army of faith—love, unity, purpose, relationship. Strange that even unwittingly to those involved, these soldiers were affirming what God intends for His children. The prayer of Jesus in John 17 embraces and encourages the very same relational patterns.

However, during the hour-long program, the single statement that grabbed my attention was, "We were never trained for defeat." That is certainly God's plan for His spiritual army in the daily conflicts each of us encounter. My mind immediately jumped from Scripture to Scripture. For our reflection, here are a few of the reassuring and encouraging passages. From the prophet Isaiah to John the beloved apostle to Paul the scholarly missionary, the message resounds with clarity. We were never trained for defeat!

Perhaps if you have a moment, you can meditate on one or all of these verses—and give God praise for the strength and grace He provides.

> *"For everyone who has been born of God overcomes the world. And this is the victory that has overcome the world—even our faith"* (1 John 5:4, ESV).

> *"No, in all these things we are more than conquerors through Him who loved us"* (Romans 8:37, ESV).

> *"But thanks be to God! He gives us the victory through our Lord Jesus Christ"* (1 Corinthians 15:57, NIV).

> *"Submit yourselves therefore to God. Resist* (military term) *the devil, and he will flee from you"* (James 4:7, ESV, explanation mine).

> *"For I can do everything through Christ, who gives me strength"* (Philippians 4:13, NLT).

"When the enemy shall come in like a flood, the Spirit of the Lord shall lift up a standard against him" (Isaiah 59:19, KJV). Note: Some translators/commentators indicate that the comma should be after the word "in," thus reading, "When the enemy shall come in, like a flood the Spirit of the Lord shall lift up a standard against him." Either way, we have the victory!

"But you belong to God, my dear children. You have already won a victory over these people, because the Spirit who lives in you is greater than the spirit who lives in the world" (1 John 4:4, NLT).

And many, many others could be cited.

As children of God, saved by the sacrifice of Christ on the cross, forgiven and restored to a right relationship with the Father, filled with the Holy Spirit—we have not been "trained for defeat"!

THERE IS ONLY ONE GOD, ETERNAL AND ALMIGHTY!

All creation, including Satan and his demonic minions, is subject to His sovereign authority.

YOU BELONG TO GOD—HE IS YOUR FATHER.

He will never abandon you or cast you aside. He has a perfect plan for your life that includes overcoming sin/evil, defeating the tempter in the name of Jesus, and having inner joy and peace.

Oh, did I forget to mention there will be battles? Many of them.

The war is not over after one skirmish. The enemy is relentless. Satan has one goal: *"to steal and kill and destroy"*—Jesus said so (John 10:10). But the remainder of that same verse offers assurance of victory. *"I came that they might have life, and that they may have it more abundantly"* (MEV)!

> You cannot have victory without struggles. Don't be surprised or taken off guard when the evil enemy comes against you.

To be certain, some of the conflicts may seem (to the natural mind) unwinnable. We cannot envision the intermediate activities between this precise moment and the end of the war. But we do know the ultimate conclusion. Paul said it so very well. *"As for me, my life has already been poured out as an offering to God. The time of my death is near. I have fought the good fight, I have finished the race, and I have remained faithful. And now the prize awaits me—the crown of righteousness, which the Lord, the righteous Judge, will give me on the day of his return"* (2 Timothy 4:6–8, NLT).

At this very moment, you may be hunkered down, listening to the rockets screaming overhead, bombs exploding with deafening sound, and sniper bullets zinging near your head. The situation may seem absolutely hopeless. But you will be victorious in/through the Heavenly Triune support team and the fellow soldiers in Christ who have joined this fierce battle with you.

You were never trained for defeat!

MY THOUGHTS:

GRASSHOPPER MENTALITY

The scriptural account of the twelve spies that Moses sent to scout out the Promised Land (Numbers 13) is known to almost everyone, even those who have only an indifferent familiarity with Old Testament revelation. So I will not reiterate the details. The ten spies who delivered a negative report to the people of Israel made a statement that basically resulted in the forty-year stint in the wilderness: "*We seemed to ourselves like grasshoppers*" (v. 33, ESV). Joshua and Caleb (the two spies who stood against the negative attitude of the other ten spies) did not dispute the fact that they had encountered giants (v. 28) or, for that matter, that these descendants of Anak saw them as grasshoppers. What they did not accept was the attitude of self-imposed helplessness and defeat—even before they attempted to cross into this God-promised land.

God had already proven Himself with numerous miracles, not the least of which was the Israelites' crossing the Red Sea on dry land and Pharaoh's army drowning

> The Israelites had enough faith to leave Egypt but not enough faith to cross the Jordan River into the land of promise.

when the walls of water collapsed on them (Exodus 14:21–31). This vast nomadic multitude was provided daily food and water, as well as guidance "*by day in a pillar of cloud*" and *"by night in a pillar of fire to give them light"* (13:21, ESV). The Scripture explains that with these supernatural provisions they could travel by day or night. Some scholars believe that the cloud shielded them from the scorching heat of the day and the fire warmed them from the frigid temperatures of the night. In short, the Deliverer was providing both provision and protection. Now, they were only days away from the fulfillment of God's promise to Abraham and his descendants (Genesis 13:14–17). But they faltered. Their tribal leaders (the ten spies) persuaded their companies that conquering this giant-infested land was utterly impossible. And consequently, they wandered in the wilderness for forty years—one year for each day that these faithless spies were in Canaan!

As with many biblical truths that are taken far beyond the intent and meaning of Scripture, some erroneous teachings have rather loudly declared that if we simply "confess" something, it will be ours to enjoy. Numerous extremes become a very real possibility when considering the matter of confession.

Let's remember these undeniable truths of Scripture:

- God is sovereign. I cannot command Him by declaring what He should or should not do.

- God is all wise. He alone knows/understands the end from the beginning. His plan is right and perfect!

- My desire/will is not preeminent. Submission to His righteous plan is the highest level of faith.

- Faith requires obedient action, not just speaking certain words with my own predetermined outcome in mind.

On the other side of that same discussion, realizing that we are prone to hearing the booming voices of faithless influences, both at the spirit level and through experiential circumstances, perhaps an inventory of how we actually view ourselves would be helpful. In our ongoing struggles, these foundational truths are reminders that assist us in achieving absolute confidence in the Almighty God.

- Those who know Christ have been "delivered" from "Egyptian captivity"—redeemed by the sacrifice of our Lord on the cross. The greatest of all miracles has already taken place in our lives. Depraved, helpless, hopeless, slaves to sin were the descriptive terms of our condition before Christ rescued us. (Read Ephesians 1:3–14 and 2:1–10.)

- From that day forward, God has been my Father, Christ Jesus my Elder Brother, and the Holy Spirit my constant Companion and Guide. Additionally, all of heaven's support personnel (angels) are prepared in an instant to function in our behalf.

- Countless times His protection and provision have covered my spirit, soul, and body. More than likely, there have been numerous times when I was not even aware of His supernatural intervention on my behalf.

- Grace has come in abundant supply for every occasion when I was unable to stand and face an uncertain future in my own ability and strength.

- This present environment is not my permanent residence. I am only a pilgrim, a noncitizen who is simply passing through. I have a short-term visa for this world! I belong to the kingdom of light, so the kingdom of darkness does not control me.

So do we worry or fret? Run and hide from reality? Live in fear of what might happen today or tomorrow? Assume that the difficult circumstances of the moment cannot be miraculously changed? Do we ever wish that we were back in Egypt for the onions, cucumbers, leeks, and garlic? (Paltry reasons for wanting to return to Egyptian bondage!)

- Indeed, the strong hand of the Lord is upon us!

- His promises will never fail.

- His covenant is immutable.

- He will never abandon His own children.

Look the enemy directly in the eye, and rebuke him in the authority of Jesus' name! *"Resist* (military terminology) *the devil, and he will flee from you"* (James 4:7, NLT; see also 1 Peter 5:8–9).

> You are not a grasshopper in God's sight, don't be one in your own.

One more thought: The giant descendants of Anak (comparable to the evil ones of this generation) may see believers as little grasshoppers. In truth, we are no match for the demonic minions of Satan in our own abilities and strength. Let's frequently repeat the words the shepherd boy David told the giant Goliath: *"You come to me with sword, spear, and javelin, but I come to you in the name of the Lord of Heaven's Armies—the God of the armies of Israel, whom you have defied"* (1 Samuel 17:45, NLT, emphasis mine). David recognized the enormous size of the giant, the large powerful weapons Goliath had at his disposal, and his defiant attitude toward the armies of Israel and God, but David invoked the authority and power of a superior Commander.

And I love his response of faith and obedience. *"David quickly ran out to meet him"* (v. 48, NLT). From the natural perspective, it seemed like a recipe for certain death for this young, untrained shepherd. But David was not looking at the giant that stood before him—he was looking past this hulk of a man. He did not try to draw rational comparisons or conclusions as to size, ability, or training. He did not listen to the cursing and verbal abuse from Goliath. The inner voice was louder than the taunts of a godless enemy. David simply trusted God for victory.

And, by the way, the Promised Land is not a reference to heaven. There were many miracles but also many battles on both sides of the Jordan River. Remember, the spiritual conflict does not ultimately conclude until we have been ushered into the presence of King Jesus. Faith to grasp the reality of our position in Christ must always be a priority all along this earthly sojourn. This is not pride; rather, it speaks of the virtue of humility.

When our faith-confidence grasps who He is and who we have become, as well as the magnitude of our miraculous deliverance from captivity, we rise above a grasshopper mentality and with bold action cross the swollen Jordan to possess the God-promised and God-assured inheritance!

Let us go up *at once*! We are well able to possess the land!

MY THOUGHTS:

JESUS: A HUMAN JUST LIKE US

The concept of *Fully God—Fully Man* is simply beyond our limited comprehension. The human mind, restricted by the fall (what a lie Satan devised, and Adam and Eve believed it!), can readily accept one or the other, but for the God to become a man like us and yet retain His eternal deity is inexplicable in human terminology. Words that we frequently use during the Christmas season, such as virgin birth or incarnation (the personification of a deity), require a high level of faith in the one true God. Yet for those who accept the Word of God as the inspired Word of God to man, there is verifiable evidence of its veracity. The course of human history revolves around the birth of this one baby boy.

The words of the angel Gabriel to Mary: *"'You will conceive and give birth to a son, and you will name him Jesus. He will be very great and will be called the Son of the Most High.'...Mary asked the angel, 'But how can this happen? I am a virgin.' The angel replied, 'The Holy Spirit will come upon you and the power of the Most High will overshadow you. So the baby to be born will be holy, and he will be called the Son of God'"* (Luke 1:31–35, NLT).

You have to admire Joseph who, in faith, accepted the word of the angel. *"Do not be afraid to take Mary as your wife. For the child within her was conceived by* the Holy Spirit. And she will have a son, and you are to name him Jesus, for he will save his people from their sins" (Matthew 1:20–21, NLT). Matthew further amplifies that this miraculous event is a direct fulfillment of Old Testament prophecy: "The virgin will conceive a child! She will give birth to a son, and they will call him Immanuel, which means 'God is with us'" (v. 23, NLT, emphasis mine, quoted from Isaiah 7:14).

Many other Scriptures verify that Jesus the man is the eternal God. One of my personal favorites is contained in the opening verses of John's Gospel. "In the beginning was the Word, and the Word was with God, and the Word was God. The same was in the beginning with God" (John 1:1–2, KJV). Further, John elaborates, "And the Word was made flesh, and dwelt among us, (and we beheld his glory, the glory as of the only begotten of the Father,) full of grace and truth" (v. 14, KJV).

So why was it so difficult for the Jewish religious leaders to accept Jesus? Weren't they looking for Messiah? Even His own chosen disciples were often confused. Why? Because they saw Jesus as a man—just like them. They were waiting for the Messiah who would dramatically deliver them from oppression and reestablish the "Kingdom," which had been nonexistent since the Babylonian captivity approximately six hundred years before Christ was born. They did not understand the "babe in the manger" when they desired a conquering king! Luke records that Jesus called Himself the "Son of Man" more than twenty times. The book of Hebrews, written to Jewish believers to show that Christ is "better" than the previous covenant of Law, refers to the Son of God as "this man" four times.

This is the important truth: He became one of us. And His earthly years were for the very specific purpose of purchasing our redemption. The Sinless One took our sins—He paid the whole of our horrible debt to a holy God. It is the only way; Jesus was the only one qualified to bring man into restored fellowship with the Father.

"For God made Christ, who never sinned, to be the offering for our sin, so that we could be made right with God through Christ" (2 Corinthians 5:21, NLT).

"And you know that Jesus came to take away our sins, and there is no sin in him" (1 John 3:5, NLT).

Now, let's fast-forward approximately two thousand years. It is much easier for us who live today to accept Jesus Christ as the Son of God than as the Son of Man. Why? The reverse of what the disciples saw is true today. We have not seen Jesus the man. It is rather difficult for us to relate to His humanity as we do not know Him as weary, hungry, disappointed, or even angry. Since we know the glorious outcome of His time on earth—sinless life, substitutionary death on the cross, victorious resurrection, ascension, and presently interceding at the Father's right hand in our behalf—He is the blessed Son of God. And that He is indeed! Fully God!

Still, there is another, often unspoken benefit from His humanity. Jesus understands the whole human scene. He knows exactly how we feel! *"So then, since we have a great High Priest who has entered heaven, Jesus the Son of God, let us hold firmly to what we believe. This High Priest of ours understands our weaknesses, for he faced all of the same testings we do, yet he did not sin"* (Hebrews 4:14–15, NLT). The babe in a cold animal stable, fleeing from a cruel despot by night into another nation, the daily grind of a family with only modest income, the rejection of family and friends—Jesus was right there. He experienced all those things! Remember, He was "moved with compassion" on the people with whom He lived (Matthew 9:36; Mark 6:34; Luke 19:41–42; etc.). And He has not forgotten all the hurts and pain of the human heart in the twenty-first century. Calling out in distress to our Heavenly Intercessor pulls at His heartstrings. He knows—and He cares!

> The ministry of Christ was not completed with His death and resurrection.
>
> Now He is seated at the Father's right hand as our heavenly intercessor.

Let's put the revealed plan of God in perspective. Jesus came to the earth in a human body, as a baby boy. A human, just like us. Understanding how Christ restricted His deity while living here as a man is the difficult part. Realistically, it is doubtful if even the most theologically astute minds can offer a satisfactory explanation. I must simply accept that God is God and know that His purpose for becoming one of us was exclusively for our deliverance from the bondage/curse of sin. For all that His brief years on earth encompassed, we should be most grateful. Our redemption/restoration to fellowship with the Father is totally dependent on His earthly experience.

Those thirty-three years are but a minor blip even on the screen of human time. He is from everlasting to everlasting. The Infinite One, which the finite human mind is incapable of absorbing. But when He returns to earth again, it will be as the conquering Lord—King of kings and Lord of lords! Alive in a glorified resurrected body. And *we shall be like him; for we shall see him as he is*" (1 John 3:2, KJV).

Jesus became the Son of Man so that
we could become the sons of God!

MY THOUGHTS:

GOD FOUND ME...IN THE DOCTOR'S OFFICE!

There were only six chairs in the tiny waiting room. This was the staging area for the men who were waiting each day for their radiation treatment. Since each of the patients had a regularly scheduled time for the nine-week period, the men whose treatment was in the same time frame soon became acquainted with each other. Conversation was casual but almost always turned to the subject of cancer. There is something breathtakingly traumatic about realizing that you are now included among those whose body has been invaded with malignant cell growth.

But this one morning was rather unique. Only two other men were waiting in the room when I arrived. One of them was there every day, and I had grown to know him quite well. He was from Thailand, and my wife and I had served there for almost five years. However, I had not seen the other man before. He was new to our group. After the man from Thailand was called for his treatment, the other gentleman and I engaged in small talk. In a moment he moved across the small room and sat in a chair beside me.

"When the Holy Ghost comes on me, He shows me things," he stated rather matter-of-factly. He continued by saying, "Let's get to the bottom line." He took my hand and began to prophetically speak words of encouragement for both the present moment and future ministry. He could not have known the major emotional struggles that I was facing at that moment. The transition from our delightful ministry in Bangkok to uncertainty about the coming days of service was a giant challenge for my mind to peacefully accept.

I pause to say that the Word of God is real, and objectively I am fully confident in the absolute truth of *all* His promises. However, being *subjectively* involved in the moment forces us to grip even harder to our faith. The words of encouragement from one of His faithful children offered great assurance and strength.

Back to the story: This stranger then stood up and said, "I have some of the Lord's money that He is directing me to give to you." I strongly protested. But he insisted. "This is the Lord's money, and He wants me to give it to you." He then handed me three $100 bills. As I was called into the treatment room, he said, "I do not usually come at this time of the day, and I did not know why I was here today—until now."

To my knowledge I have not seen the man since that day.

The fallout from this experience was powerful. The reassurance of the Lord's guidance was emotionally stabilizing. Of course, any of us appreciate financial blessings. However, to me the most significant aspect of that morning was that the Lord knew *exactly* where I was—sitting in a tiny waiting room in a cancer center. And He cared enough to arrange for one of His children to be there at that precise moment.

Actually, this should not be considered unusual. After all, we are His children—the children of a loving, caring heavenly Father. By the way, He knows exactly where you are both physically and emotionally at this very moment in your faith walk. Perhaps He "found" you today with this testimony.

"Casting all your cares [all your anxieties, all your worries, and all your concerns, once and for all] on Him, for He cares about you [with deepest affection, and watches over you very carefully]" (1 Peter 5:7, AMPC).

"Trust in the Lord and do good...

Take delight in the Lord...

Commit everything you do to the Lord...

Be still in the presence of the Lord, and wait patiently for him to act."

(Psalm 37:3–5, 7, NLT)

MY THOUGHTS:

A Heart Like Your Heart, Lord

H.M.L.

H. MAURICE LEDNICKY
Arr. by Nate Carter

Give me a heart like Your heart, O Lord, I pray;

A heart that is brok - en for one who's gone as - tray
A heart ruled by love___ when there's a bet - ter way.

Let me nev - er grow___ cal - loused by the things I have seen,
Let me not re - mem - ber wrongs___ that have come my___ way,

But have a heart of com - pas - sion for a broth - er in need.
But have a heart of for - give - ness that's___ soft - ened by Thee.

OVERTHINKING...

Overthinking—an intriguing word that captured my attention recently. Without "overthinking" it, I saw two possible distinct yet related meanings: (1) microscopically searching for every minute nuance, parsing every syllable, or (2) the inability or unwillingness to resolutely make a decision and then move forward based on that conclusion.

But this concept has a spiritual perspective that is worthy of further consideration.

First, it should be agreed that faith and intellect are not mutually exclusive. Those who insist that man's finite rational capabilities can identify/comprehend the infinite wisdom of the Sovereign are as foolish as those who would admonish worshippers to "leave your brain at the door" when you come into God's house. There is ample scriptural evidence to discount both extremes.

"Come now, and let us reason together, says the Lord" (Isaiah 1:18, MEV, emphasis mine). The implication is that of a court in which both sides are allowed to present the facts of the case.

> *"Oh, how great are God's riches and wisdom and knowledge! How impossible it is for us to understand his decisions and his ways!"* (Romans 11:33, NLT, emphasis mine).

The experience of Moses at the burning bush (Exodus 3–4) serves as a rather graphic illustration of overthinking God's specific direction. Of course, we recognize that Moses did not have any of the written Word as a means to assure verification for this encounter. For us, the Word of God must always be the primary source of evaluation for personal direction. Coupled with the Holy Spirit's illumination/application of the Word, it is not unreasonable to believe that a high level of confidence can be attained as we are traveling the unique path He has ordained.

In reviewing the encounter of Moses with the preincarnate Christ on Mt. Horeb, four major questions come into focus.

1. FRACTURED IDENTITY: WHO AM I? (EXODUS 3:11)

Moses had suffered a severe blow to his confidence. He had been raised in the palace of the ruling pharaoh with all its material advantages yet taught the principles of Jehovah by a godly mother. These two diametrically opposite lifestyles vied for his young attention, acceptance, and affection. Such inner conflict must have been quite a challenge in the emotional/intellectual/spiritual development of Moses. Then, when he assumed he had chosen God's way, it all came crashing down on him. Fleeing from what had been the security of the palace, he lived the next forty years tending sheep. By the way, the Egyptians despised shepherds (Genesis 46:34). That was a steep drop—from having multiple servants who would immediately come at the snap of his fingers to tending a bunch of dumb sheep.

Now, the bush is on fire and not being consumed. In this holy moment God tells Moses that He will send him to deliver Israel from Egypt. Remember, from the time of Joseph until that day, Israel had been under Egyptian domination for more than four hundred years. Perhaps the answer Moses gave should not be considered too unusual. No doubt those dramatic moments in Egypt had tantalized his mind for these forty years—he overthought it! Can you imagine his internal conflict? "I tried and failed miserably. Why would God ask such a miserable failure to be His spokesperson? Me, stand up against Pharaoh? It could never happen!"

It is not a stretch to conclude that many today would see themselves as unqualified to step out in faith/obedience in response to the claims of Christ. At one point they enthusiastically started on the faith journey, but something derailed them. Emotional chaos ensued. Trusted friends walked away. The bottom dropped out. Self-expectations were shattered. Totally confused/disillusioned. Nothing to do except retreat and hide in shame and solitude. Surely God was so disappointed that even He would look in another direction to find a more suitable replacement.

Thankfully, that is not the God we serve. He is filled with compassion, mercy, and grace. One bad decision does not negate His love. So if you find yourself asking, "Who am I?" remember you are a redeemed child of God. Not perfect (no one is) but keenly aware of the intercessory ministry of Christ at the Father's right hand. Quickly run back to Him, never away from Him. Do not allow Satan to keep pushing the negative thoughts of failure back to the front of your mind. In short, don't overthink it! Be restored in Jesus' name.

2. AUTHORITATIVE AUTHENTICITY: Who are you? (Exodus 3:13)

Moses was really at the bottom. Now, he was even questioning the reality and authority of the Sovereign God. This was more than just a fleeting doubt brought on by the magnitude of what he was being told. On the backside of the desert, Moses had hours/days/years to repeatedly replay the injustice suffered by God's people. If God were God, why did this suffering go on and on and on? He overthought it!

It's a frequent question among both believers and unbelievers alike. Why do bad things happen to good people? If God is really all powerful, why all the injustice in the world? Why do the innocent face famine, disease, and death? The implications are frightening: (1) God is deemed to be less than His Word declares Him to be, or (2) worse,

He is judged as the originator of evil in the world. Those deceitful thoughts are instigated by the evil one. Satan tried (and succeeded) to deceive Adam and Eve in the Garden of Eden. He was bold enough to assume (foolishly) that he could attempt the same intimidating tactic with the Son of God. *"If you are the Son of God..."* (Matthew 4:3, 6).

Some basic axioms, when appropriately applied, will quell this erroneous, faith-destroying thought process:

- The created is never equal to the Creator (Romans 9:20–21).

- God's moral creation (angels and men) were given the power of choice, a free will to accept or reject the relationship offered with the Father, provided through Christ the Redeemer.

- God has a master plan, established in love, that is consistent with His sovereign nature/authority. He is absolute in every respect and never changes!

- God is infinite; man is finite. God alone has neither beginning nor ending. Time restrictions are earthly. Eternity is heavenly.

- For God to superimpose His absolute perfection upon all creation would violate His design for the creature (made in His own image) to voluntarily worship and serve Him. God's eternal desire is for all of His creation to be willing servants, not coerced slaves.

All of God is all of God—He is!

Accepting God for who He is and what He does is foundational to scriptural faith.

"And without faith it is impossible to please God, for he who comes to God must believe that He exists and that He is a rewarder of those who diligently seek Him" (Hebrews 11:6, MEV).

The truth is that none of us will ever understand/comprehend God. After all, His ways are *"past finding out"* (Romans 11:33, KJV).

One scriptural truth—easily spoken but very difficult to actualize—that will settle this issue in our hearts is *trust*.

The highest level of faith is trust.

Confident trust when there is no glimmer of light on the pathway demands faith of great magnitude. *"'Tis so sweet to trust in Jesus, just to take Him at His word..."* Don't overthink it. When you have exhausted all your intellectual capabilities, human logic, and cultural conclusion, God will still be God!

3. HYPOTHETICAL SCENARIO: WHAT IF? (EXODUS 4:1)

Moses is way ahead of himself now. He is playing the "What if?" game. He is doing much more than looking at possibilities and being prepared for future contingencies. Moses wants to have the answers before the questions arise—a classic example of overthinking. Fortunately for him, God is patient! Remember, this is a conversation with the preincarnate Christ in a moment so profound that Moses was told to take off his shoes. This was a sacred encounter in a holy place. Moses, God is asking for your obedience and assuring you that His plan will be completed!

Fear is the antithesis of faith. It is paralyzing to obedient action. The humorous story is told of an unmarried lady sitting by the street and crying profusely. Her friend saw her and rushed over to ask what had happened. Sobbing, the lady replied, "I was just thinking, what if I were married and had a child and she ran out into the street and a car ran over her and she was killed? How awful it would be!". Have we ever been equally absurd with our faith? *"Fret not"* (Psalm 37:1, KJV). Fret is an excellent synonym for worry—worry to the point of an all-consuming preoccupation with possibilities. Perhaps that is the extreme side. However, how many believers fail to take any forward steps of faith, using various methods of rationalization for delaying an obedient response/action? Excuses often become total disobedience.

Hold to His steady hand. Our living/ loving Lord would not ask us to go unless He was certain we could get there. "Yes, Lord" is the only correct answer. Don't overthink it.

> The walk of faith will never become a walk of sight.

4. PERSONAL LIMITATIONS: WHY ME? CAN'T YOU SEE I'M NOT QUALIFIED? (EXODUS 4:10)

To be openly honest, the Lord has never asked me to do anything that I "felt" qualified to do. To assume personal qualification is dangerous in the arena of pride and self-reliance, and almost inevitably produces an undesired consequence. But back to Moses. It may seem that we are being excessively hard on him. This thought process did not suddenly appear out of nowhere. He had been thinking about the events in Egypt that drove him to hide for his life for forty years. I have no idea if he ever even imagined that God might personally speak to him. What we do know is that in a matter of minutes, Moses unloaded every frustration of those painful years. And his conclusion was rather straightforward: "God, I can't do this!" "*Lord, please send someone else*" (Exodus 4:13, ESV, emphasis mine).

Lingering disappointments, especially when we sincerely tried to do what was right, can severely cloud our thinking. Our motives were pure but critically challenged. The situation did not rectify itself. After our inability (or unwillingness) to release the devastating hurt, playing it over and over again, the pain increasingly takes on a new, deeper dimension. The spirit is wounded. To retreat and suffer in silence seems to be the only solution. Then comes the eruption of emotion: "God, I can't do this!" Satan wants us to keep on reliving all that is unjust and unfair. If he can just get us to overthink the situation, our whole outlook on life will be marred, scarred, and damaged. The Psalmist said it correctly: "*I look up to the mountains—does my help come from *there? My help comes from the Lord, who made heaven and earth! He will not let you stumble; the one who watches over you will not slumber"* (Psalm 121:1–3, NLT).

So what is worth daily repetition?

1. God is still God!
2. We are His children!
3. Life is not always fair!
4. Trust in the Sovereign Lord in every circumstance!
5. His love, mercy, grace, and goodness will provide joy and peace!

"And now, dear brothers and sisters, one final thing. Fix your thoughts on what is true, and honorable, and right, and pure, and lovely, and admirable. Think about things that are excellent and worthy of praise" (Philippians 4:8, NLT).

MY THOUGHTS:

PENTECOSTAL TRADITION

Perhaps it is only semantics; however, I have a nagging uneasiness about trying to couple the words Pentecostal and tradition together. Not wanting to overreact, I consulted the dictionary for the common usage/definition of the word tradition.

Tradition: "the handing down orally of stories, beliefs and customs...; a long-established custom or practice that has the effect of an unwritten law...; among Christians, the unwritten teachings regarded as handed down from Jesus and the apostles" (By the way, the same was said of Jewish and Muslim.)

The message of Pentecost is not unwritten! It is fully and clearly confirmed in the inspired Word of God. Luke, who wrote both the Gospel and the book of Acts, closed the Gospel and began Acts with the teaching of Christ concerning the Holy Spirit.

> *"And now I will send the Holy Spirit, just as my Father promised. But stay here in the city (Jerusalem) until the Holy Spirit comes and fills you with power from heaven"* (Luke 24:49, NLT).

> *"He commanded them, 'Do not leave Jerusalem until the Father sends you the gift he promised you, as I told you before. John baptized with water, but in*

just a few days you will be baptized with the Holy Spirit'" (Acts 1:4–5, NLT).

In Jesus' final discourse with the disciples prior to the cross, John records a very explicit/detailed discussion of the coming Holy Spirit (John 13–16). Knowing that His death on the cross was in the immediate future, Jesus was giving instruction but was also providing comfort and assurance for the coming days. The men who were to become the very foundation of the New Testament church were not left to speculate. Jesus was emphatic about the importance of this message—a fuller revelation of the power and working of the Holy Spirit in the world, church, and individual believer. Experiential evidence is documented in Scripture of those who received the Holy Spirit in the infant church. In Acts 2, 10, and 19, the Scripture explicitly states that these believers "spoke in tongues." In Acts 8 and 9, there is strong evidence to believe that these believers also spoke in tongues. In the case of Paul (Acts 9), he confirms to the church at Corinth that he "spoke in tongues" frequently (1 Corinthians 12–14). From its inception the New Testament church (in which we are included) was a Spirit-filled community of faith! This is not simply an oral tradition that has been communicated through the centuries by word of mouth.

> Every believer must have a personal Pentecostal experience to fully know and declare its scriptural veracity.

> The longer one goes without an experience, the easier it becomes to deny its authenticity.

The passing of time, the fear (at times valid) of extremism/emotionalism, the lack of pulpit proclamation, the desire for cultural relevance, etc., etc., all create an atmosphere in which a gradual erosion of the vitality and urgency of the Pentecostal experience for every born-again follower of Christ begins to develop. It is somewhat like a sinkhole that suddenly opens up at a moment when no one expected it or anticipated the damage it would create.

So, for me personally, I want to unequivocally reaffirm that I am a Pentecostal—not in name/tradition only, but by the experience that is part and parcel of the New Testament doctrine/truth. The infilling (baptism) with the Spirit, the gifts of the Spirit, and the fruit of the Spirit are all explicitly revealed in the written Word of God. Generational concepts, cultural mores, or theological bantering do not diminish or alter inspired Scripture.

For the sake of clarity, the baptism in the Holy Spirit is only the beginning of the Spirit-filled life. It is in no way a conclusion or the zenith of spiritual life. Being Pentecostal is a daily walk in the Spirit (Galatians 5) that begins with accepting and receiving the "promise of the Father."

As we rapidly approach the nearness of our Lord's return (both the rapture of the church and then His earthly return/revelation) and the minions of hell are unleashed in an unprecedented manner in the end-time context, this is certainly not the time to downplay the significance of personally receiving/appropriating the power of the Holy Spirit. The church, headed by our Lord, has always been and always will be countercultural. For this to be present reality, it is imperative that we embrace the fullness of the Spirit, both individually and collectively.

The Spirit affords many individual enablements that are so desperately needed to live in spiritual victory and receive the fullness of God's provisions/promises. However, it is of the highest priority if we are to obey the command of our Lord to be His witnesses!

"But you shall receive power when the Holy Spirit comes upon you. And you shall be My witnesses in Jerusalem, and in all Judea and Samaria, and to the ends of the earth" (Acts 1:8, MEV).

Be filled with the Spirit. Jesus is coming for His bride (church) very soon!

NON-GMO

Did you ever wonder about the numbers on the little stickers that are on fresh fruit? Without going into a long discussion, all of them have a four-digit code— usually beginning with the number 3 or 4. This indicates the fruit was "conventionally" grown, using fertilizer, pesticides, and other potentially harmful measures to project the trees or vines.

There are two exceptions to this standard numbering— the addition of an 8 or 9 at the front of the numerical code. An 8 is of major concern as it means the produce has been genetically modified. The 9 verifies that the fruit is organically grown.

Back to "genetically modified" for a moment. A simple definition: an organism not naturally found in nature is scientifically altered, and a new DNA is created. According to the most recent literature, corn, soy, and cotton are the biggest culprits in the USA. The stated purpose is to enhance development and growth.

"Organically grown" is determined by strict standards, which include no added growth hormones or steroids (animals) no synthetic fertilizers or dangerous

> Long since I have concluded that any spiritual growth— or decline—is primarily and proportionally measured by our approach to and appropriation of His Word.

53

pesticides (fruit and vegetables). The jury is still out as to whether the significant cost increase outweighs any long-term physical hazards.

The specific intent of this discussion is to neither champion physical health (although our bodies are the "temple of the Holy Spirit") nor applaud/condemn scientific procedures. In the language of the New Testament, this is a parable (illustration) contrasting the "pure" seed with the "genetically modified" seed. In one of His widely known teaching sessions, Jesus spoke of the sower and the seed to the agri-economic culture of that day. And He specifically noted the seed was the Word of God (Luke 8:11). While the preaching/teaching emphasis on this parable is frequently on the one who sows the seed and/or the types of soil on which the seed is scattered, the quality of the seed is never questioned. But perhaps for this moment we should narrow our focus to carefully consider what is being sown, as well as understand the who and the where.

SOME OBSERVATIONS...

First, and of utmost significance, the Word of God is divinely inspired. Amazing how many people, even numbered among believers, do not accept the written Word as being "God breathed."

Every Scripture is God-breathed (given by His inspiration) and profitable for instruction, for reproof and conviction of sin, for correction of error and discipline in obedience, [and] for training in righteousness (in holy living, in conformity to God's will in thought, purpose, and action) (2 Timothy 3:16, AMPC).

Above all, you must realize that no prophecy in Scripture ever came from the prophet's own understanding, or from human initiative. No, those prophets were moved by the Holy Spirit, and they spoke from God (2 Peter 1:20–21, NLT).

This encompasses all of the Word—both Old and New Testaments!

> The beginning point from which all spiritual deception, doctrinal error, and unscriptural behavior emanates is to deny that all or portions of God's written Word are inspired, infallible truth.

The liberty to "pick and choose" what you want to accept or reject immediately negates the entire concept of inspiration. In effect, this is changing the DNA of Scripture—it becomes genetically modified!

Then, another dangerous thought process relates to the authority of the Word. Both Old and New Testaments give explicit evidence to the inherent power of the Word.

For the word of God is alive and powerful. It is sharper than the sharpest two-edged sword, cutting between soul and spirit, between joint and marrow. It exposes our innermost thoughts and desires (Hebrews 4:12, NLT).

Prophets of old stood before kings and rulers boldly declaring, "Thus saith the Lord..." Literally, they risked their lives on the authority of what God told them. Jesus taught that not one dotting of an *i* or crossing of a *t* would fail until it was all fulfilled (Matthew 5:18). To conclude, for example, that miracles have ceased is to imply that generational or cultural changes lessen the authority of Scripture. This, too, alters the seed—it is genetically modified!

Perhaps (in my personal opinion) the most insidious and dangerous modification of the Word looming before us in this generation/culture is the almost unrestrained acceptance of contemporary mores as a basis for redefining scriptural truth (i.e., homosexuality as an acceptable lifestyle for a believer, the inclusion of various elements of other religions and humanistic philosophies, etc.). The theme of cultural relevance has often been trumpeted so loudly that it diminishes or, even more damaging, overrides an unwavering commitment to the Word. In spite of proclaiming otherwise, the method has at times changed the message. Anecdotal evidence has been employed to challenge generally understood and accepted scriptural doctrine.

Personal experience does not alter the immutable principles of the Word.

This transition comes rather easily when the subjective reality is defined by human intellect. Man's concept of fairness and justice run counter to the absolute perfection of the Sovereign God. To use experience as a measuring device for interpreting the Word inevitably results in scriptural genetic modification! Rather than looking for loopholes in Scripture to justify our carnal/sinful behavior and attitudes, *now* is the moment to take up the "sword of the Spirit" (Word of God) (Ephesians 6:17).

Intolerance toward true followers of Christ has reached a crescendo in this era. There is a worldwide attack. At its core this is not culturally or politically motivated—it is the highest level of spiritual espionage and aggression. The Old Testament prophets were executed because they refused to "genetically modify" the commands of the Lord. John the Baptist had his head served on a platter for offending an adulterous woman. Paul suffered all types of physical abuse and ultimately death for his unwavering declaration that Jesus Christ is God's Son. These scriptural personalities, along with many who have lived in the centuries following, were not superhuman heroes. They were ordinary men and women with an uncompromising conviction that the Word of God was worth defending—in life or death.

It is more than just a catchy phrase—

The Word says what it means and means what it says!

FREEDOM'S JUST ANOTHER WORD

In 1969, Kris Kristofferson wrote a pungent song of the era titled "Me and Bobby McGee." Janis Joplin, who died in 1970 of an overdose at age 27, made the song a worldwide phenomenon. It has been recorded across the lines of every genre of music, from Johnny Cash to the Grateful Dead. One line from the song captured my attention years ago while I was serving in youth ministry. I had not thought of this song for many years. Recently, however, during my devotional time, these few lyrics traced across my mind: "Freedom's just another word for nothing left to lose..."

The scriptural passage I was reading is Romans 6:6–7: *"We know that our old sinful selves were crucified with Christ so that sin might lose its power in our lives. We are no longer slaves to sin. For when we died with Christ we were set free from the power of sin"* (NLT). Paul uses the expression "free from the power of sin" three times in this one chapter, emphasizing this powerful truth to the Roman believers.

Jesus spoke to a group of Jewish people who had just accepted His teaching, *"You are truly my disciples if you remain faithful to my teachings. And you will <u>know the truth</u>, and the <u>truth will set you free</u>"* (John 8:31–32, NLT, emphasis mine). They did not understand the idea of freedom, so the Lord explained further. *"I tell you the truth, everyone who sins is a slave of sin. A slave is not a permanent*

57

member of the family, but a son is part of the family forever. *So if the Son sets you free, you are truly free*" (vv. 34–36, NLT, emphasis mine).

While "Me and Bobby McGee" has absolutely nothing to do with God or faith in Him, the particular lyrics that stood out to me do express a deep theological concept.

Salvation…"*So now there is no condemnation for those who belong to Christ Jesus. And because you belong to him, the power of the life-giving Spirit has freed you from the power of sin that leads to death*" (Romans 8:1–2, NLT). How gloriously amazing! Free from ALL the guilt of the past. Clean, pure, justified before a holy God. Nothing left to lose.

Sanctification…"*Since you have heard about Jesus and have learned the truth that comes from him, throw off your old sinful nature and your former way of life, which is corrupted by lust and deception. Instead, let the Spirit renew your thoughts and attitudes. Put on your new nature, created to be like God—truly righteous and holy*" (Ephesians 4:21–24, NLT). Deliberately abandon the sinful nature and its destructive consequences; assimilate the new righteousness nature, filled with joy and peace. Now comes true freedom to flow in the Spirit, minus all the baggage of carnality and immaturity. Surely, nothing to lose here.

Surrender…"*And now I am bound by the Spirit to go to Jerusalem. I don't know what awaits me, except that the Holy Spirit tells me in city after city that jail and suffering lie ahead. But my life is worth nothing to me unless I use it for finishing the work assigned me by the Lord Jesus*" (Acts 20:22–24, NLT, Paul to the church elders of Ephesus).

This aspect of our faith is a lifelong challenge. Yet it is at this pivotal place that freedom is understood. Jesus fully understood His earthly mission at baptism. In spite of the heart-breaking rejection He suffered, He never wavered from the will of the Father.

> Jesus won the battle of the cross at the stone altar in Gethsemane.

58

Indeed, He endured great physical suffering after His prayer, but His surrender was complete. From my perspective each of us must have a personal Gethsemane—a crisis moment when we completely release absolutely every aspect of life to be unequivocally under the control of the Lord. The early believers, who knew the horrors of Roman crucifixion, understood the concept of *"being crucified with Christ"* (Galatians 2:20; 6:14).

The level of our commitment is not determined by how much of self we are willing to submit to the lordship of Christ; rather, it is more accurately defined by those things that we are unwilling to release.

Although it is not possible to evaluate individual hearts and emotions (and it is important that we refrain from the temptation to do so), perhaps a broad brush would identify a few areas that may pose a struggle in the spiritual process of complete surrender:

- Self-preservation, both physically and intellectually

- Creature comforts, material possessions

- Cultural acceptance and participation

- Perpetual immaturity, apathy, content with current spiritual status

- Spiritual elitism, self-reliance, judgmental spirit

- Misunderstanding of personally distinct eternal purpose

There is no standardized template to determine levels of commitment; each person has a unique place/assignment in the body of Christ. However, a valid measuring tool for personal evaluation is found in one simple statement: "No, Lord!" The two words are antithetical. It is impossible to put them together. Once we say no to the Lord, He is no longer our Lord.

> "I can't" reveals a lack of faith.

> "I won't" reveals a lack of commitment.

True spiritual freedom is "just another word for nothing left to lose."

MY THOUGHTS:

THE MESSAGE OF A PROPHET— THEN AND NOW!

Prophets of Old Testament record came from a variety of backgrounds, including economic and social status. For example, Isaiah was a first cousin to King Uzziah and was probably quite well connected in political circles. Daniel was gifted with a scholarly mind and was taken into Babylonian captivity when he was approximately 20 years of age. Jonah and Habakkuk were both men of political influence. Amos, on the other hand, was a shepherd and caretaker of wild fig trees. In several cases little or nothing is known of the family history or how the prophets came to be recognized and respected. But the message they spoke was in a broad sense quite the same. Of course, the Holy Spirit used the personality of each prophet in declaration. The writing style reflected not only the condition of the culture but also the uniqueness of the prophet's thought process. For me, it reinforces my personal belief in divine inspiration of Scripture when you put all these missives together and the end result over several hundred years reveals the same consistent word from the Almighty.

In capsule form, the seven progressive steps noted here define the ministry of the Old Testament prophet:

1. Denounces sin/evil

2. Warns of impending judgment

3. Emphasizes abandoning evil ways

4. Pleads for genuine repentance

5. Promises divine forgiveness

6. Assures restoration to grace/relationship

7. Declares future glories

Many Scriptures verify this pattern of a prophetic ministry. In the truest definition of a God-called prophet, the proclamation includes both "forth telling" and "foretelling". Realistically, the majority of Old Testament prophecies would easily rest on the forth telling side of the equation. These dynamic voices spoke about what they saw at that precise moment. Idol worship. Corrupt political systems. Immorality. Injustice. The solemn warning of impending judgment was in direct response to who/what these nations, religious leaders, or individuals had become. There was also the beautiful foretelling of the promises of future glory. It was (and is) this hope that the dedicated followers of Jehovah anticipated and longed for.

Now, let's move forward to the prophets in the New Testament church (of which we are still part today). It is important to understand that there is a clear scriptural distinction between the ministry of a prophet and the ministry of an evangelist.

• The prophet speaks directly to believers.

• The evangelist speaks directly to unbelievers.

As the majority of the New Testament (other than the four Gospels and book of Acts) is written in prose (as opposed to narrative), there are few insights into the actual ministry of the men/women anointed for the ministry of the prophet and/or evangelist. As an aside, the word "evangelists" is used three times in Scripture, all of which are in the New Testament.

In this era of grace, the prophet is the God-anointed spokesperson to the New Testament church. In our early years of ministry, we traveled as "evangelists," which more appropriately should have been called "revivalists." Our primary emphasis was speaking to believers—to call them to repentance, challenging them to turn from sin and carnality. In reality, the message for the local church was prophetic. However, in those years when the assembling of worshipers occupied a far more significant role in our culture than it does today, it was quite common for those who had not accepted Christ as Savior to attend a "revival meeting." Often unbelievers came at the strong insistence of a family member or friend. Hence, many came to know the Savior in those special services when opportunity was given for repentance (confession of sin) and declaration of faith in Christ. Still, the primary thrust was to call the church to once again experience a dramatic renewal of Holy Ghost fire and zeal.

Suffice it to say that both the prophet (revivalist) and the evangelist are greatly needed in this generation. Inevitably, when true revival permeates any body of believers, they will spontaneously begin to share the glorious message of redemption with everyone in their sphere of influence.

As an aside, the ministry gifts Christ gave to the church—apostle, prophet, evangelist, pastor, teacher—are not positions of organizational authority, nor are they ranked in degree of significance (Ephesians 4:11–16). Each occupies a strategic place in advancing the cause of Christ. Each complements the others.

The tendency of every generation, having begun in the fire of the Holy Spirit, is to

> Revival precedes evangelism. Evangelism flows out of revival.

settle comfortably into the daily benefits of His grace and subsequently become rather apathetic. This leads to a dangerous assumption of spiritual entitlement to His favor or an attitude of spiritual elitism. In turn, perhaps subtly, scripturally denounced carnality and sin creep into the body of Christ. Perhaps one could identify it as the Laodicean mentality (Revelation 3:14–22). Then arrives God's anointed prophet to warn and call for repentance and humility before the Almighty (2 Chronicles 7:14). From the earliest years of the New Testament church, the prophetic voice was crucial. Applying the Word to contemporary culture, especially in those areas where the church has adopted unscriptural attitudes and practices, is never out of order. Dare I say the need for such Spirit-anointed voices is exponentially greater in the twenty-first century!

Unfortunately, the prophet's message is not always enthusiastically received, even by professing believers. The prophet may be rejected maligned or even have his/her motives questioned. A self-justifying spirit always becomes defensive when its true nature is exposed. This was not uncommon in the Old Testament record—Jesus mentioned that the Jewish people had been guilty of extreme actions against prophets (Matthew 23:37). However, without regard to personal popularity or success, these men/women of God spoke with clarity, boldness, and courage. So it must be today! Give us a twenty-first-century Jeremiah who is brokenhearted over the sinful behavior of God's people! Give us a twenty-first-century John the Baptist who will not compromise the message.

Cynicism, despair, or resignation must never be the spiritual position of the prophet. Ezekiel was told to have a head harder than the rebellious people to whom he preached (Ezekiel 3:4–9). God's power is greater than the deceptive devices of demonic forces. The conviction of the Holy Spirit still reaches into the hidden inner chambers of the heart. The Father's love and grace are still available for everyone who calls on Him (through Christ). The Word of God confirms and reassures our faith.

Father, we pray that Your overwhelming, indisputable call will compel men/women to declare Your eternal plan "without fear or favor" in this end-time generation!

P.S. The distinction between a "major" and "minor" prophet is simply the length of the message...

MY THOUGHTS:

THE SNAKE IS IN THE GARDEN—AGAIN!

L ies. Half-truths. Deception. The story of the serpent in the previously unspoiled Garden of Eden is legendary (actually, inspired is the correct term) (Genesis 3). It was the devil's first frontal assault against God's made-in-His-own-image creation. Make no mistake, this fallen angel had bitter revenge as his motive to defeat/destroy God's purpose for expanding the circle of divine fellowship. No, the Eternal One did not need man to be complete or fulfilled; He was affording this dust-of-the-earth creation an opportunity for intimate personal fellowship with Him. That is exactly what Lucifer had enjoyed and, in his pride, falsely assumed that he and the Almighty were equals. His goal was to forcefully push the one true God aside and become the Sovereign. We know how that ended. He was cast down from heaven and given (for a temporary season) some authority over the earth.

By the way, at this very moment we are as close to hell as we ever need to be. Jesus promised He would build His church, "*and the gates of hell shall not prevail against it*" (Matthew 16:18, KJV).

So from that time forward, his tactic has been the destruction of man by deception. Lies. Half-truths. Innuendos. Intimidation. As believers, this should not shock us. According to the words of our Lord, "*he* (Satan) *is a liar and the father of lies"* (John 8:44,NLT, addition mine).

Now, if we come back to the opening chapter of Genesis, the Lord said, *"Be fruitful, and multiply, and replenish the earth"* (Genesis 1:28, KJV). Interestingly, the same expression is given to Noah and his sons following the flood (Genesis 9:1, 7). Some scholars define this as a command; others refer to it as a blessing. Either way, the intent is clear. Through the process of procreation, a man and woman were to have children and continue to populate and repopulate the earth. Remember that with disobedience came the curse of death (Genesis 3:15–19).

Where is the serpent back in the garden? Think about four deceptive lies that have been foisted on society in this generation. They have been defined as "rights"—even as God-given rights.

1. Abortion (the right to destroy a life for personal convenience)

2. LGBT (i.e., homosexuality, lesbianism, bisexuality, transgenderism)

3. Same-sex marriage (the marriage of two men or two women)

4. Sexual identity (the gender you choose to be at a given moment)

The bottom line for each of these items reveals yet another attempt by Satan to undercut the future of humanity. It is an attack on one of the Creator's first instructions: *"Be fruitful and multiply."* It is absolute perversion of the divine plan. Mankind would cease to exist if men/women ceased to reproduce children. Sound far-fetched? No two men or two women have ever or can ever bear a child. Abortion has the same effect. Over a period of time, life would become unsustainable without a significant younger generation to replace the elders who grow old and die. It would be elimination by attrition. Additionally, the emotional impact of living in such gross deception cannot be overestimated. Especially when one considers that God "*abandoned them to their shameful desires*" (Romans 1:24, 26, 28, NLT). Literally, God turned them loose!

What have the serpent and, subsequently, his "snakettes" proposed? This deviant lifestyle is the right of every person to "love" (using the term unscripturally) whomever he/she desires. We must all be tolerant (again used in an unscriptural manner) of the uniqueness of others, tolerance being defined as "you must believe my way or you are a homophobic bigot." No reasoning. No discussion. Just do not dare expect me to accept you—but you absolutely must accept me for who/what I am. Diversity, under such satanic deception, is really horrific, sinful disobedience to the truth of the Word of God.

Dear faithful followers of Christ, this *is* a big deal. It is the most serious of struggles between good/evil, between God/Satan. Never in my life of more than three quarters of a century have the lines been so clearly drawn. The picture is not abstract. No guesswork is required. The enemy's strategy is championed in bold letters. The battle is not political in essence—it is spiritual. Even the most well-planned and well-intended legislation cannot whiten a darkened heart. The powers of darkness are seizing every opportunity to discredit, diminish, and even try to destroy the church of Jesus Christ. Remember, our location is at the very "gates of hell" (Matthew 16:18). It is in this war zone that our Lord promised to build His church. This is not the hour to capitulate or suddenly fall silent or refuse to stand firm in our faith. Light and darkness have nothing in common (2 Corinthians 6:14–18). I am not suggesting any specific method of action other than earnest prayer of intercession. Fervent prayer is mandated if we are to push back the evil hordes that are relentlessly attacking from every direction. The Spirit will guide you as you walk in righteousness in your workplace or perhaps even direct you into some bold stance in the public arena. Each situation is unique. The Holy Spirit is our wise guide.

What we do know—absolutely—is that Satan has always been inferior. Christ defeated him through death and resurrection. Our King is victorious!

The battles may be fierce;

The struggles intense;

The accusations loud;

The persecution escalating.

Take out your sword (Word of God) and resist the poisonous snake in the garden!

MY THOUGHTS:

THE STRENGTH OF GENTLENESS

As Pentecostals—having experienced the personal infilling of the Holy Spirit (Acts 2:4)—we often emphasize the manifestation of the "gifts of the Spirit" as identified by the apostle Paul (1 Corinthians 12). This is both scriptural and important. These gifts were provided by the Spirit for the New Testament church—of which we are part. These supernatural gifts function horizontally, normally in an assembled body of believers, and involve two or more people. I like to call this the next progressive step in the Spirit, following the baptism in the Spirit. By the manifestation of these gifts, a particular community of believers is enriched, and spiritual growth occurs.

These specific nine gifts definitely need expression in the church in this generation!

REVELATION	POWER	UTTERANCE
Word of wisdom	Faith	Prophecy
Word of knowledge	Miracles	Tongues
Discerning of spirits	Healing	Interpretation of tongues

It is worth noting that it is the Holy Spirit who chooses both the occasion for the manifestation and the vessel (believer) to be used for the manifestation. Spirit-filled believers do not possess any of the gifts; they are resident in the Holy Spirit. Consequently, the Spirit may empower a person to be the conduit for any or all of the gifts as the need arises.

But, praise the Lord, there is more! The personal ministry of the Spirit is at work within our hearts to bring about change and continued spiritual growth/maturity. This the Word of God identifies as the "fruit of the Spirit" (Galatians 5:22–23).

RELATIONSHIP TO GOD	RELATIONSHIP TO OTHERS	RELATIONSHIP TO SELF
Love	Long-suffering (patience)	Faith (faithfulness)
Joy	Gentleness (kindness)	Meekness
Peace	Goodness	Temperance (self control)

Also written by the apostle Paul, this passage juxtaposes the fruit of the Spirit against the works of the flesh. Immediately we understand that this "fruit" is personal, progressive, involves time and effort, and ultimately produces observable change in attitude and behavior. This is the Spirit's work in the maturation of each individual. Our growth does not and cannot depend on the equal progress of other believers. This is the direct result of the vertical relationship I personally have with the one true God. The stark reality is that my spiritual maturity is in direct proportion to my desire and willingness to hear/obey.

The "fruit of the Spirit is...gentleness..." (Galatians 5:22–23, ESV). Not a specific type of personality. Not a wimpy person who refuses to ever take a position. This is the inner work of the Holy Spirit manifesting itself in the daily vicissitudes of life!

A correct understanding of what scriptural gentleness encompasses will guide our thinking. The Greek words in the New Testament for "gentleness" and "meekness" are closely related. The word used in Galatians 5:23 (*prautes*) means "to submit one's strength in a posture of meekness."

Often we can look to the negative side of an issue to more effectively point to the positive. The brief list noted here (not intended to be all inclusive) may reveal how desperately we need the Spirit's fruit of gentleness.

OPPOSITE OF GENTLENESS:

1. Always has to be right/verbally judgmental of those who have different preferences/opinions

2. Vehemently attacks every person with whom he/she disagrees

3. Speaks down to others with a harsh tone

4. Disregards the feelings of others/inconsiderate/domineering

5. Quickly finds fault/points to the negative

6. Demands unearned respect

7. Reacts angrily when challenged or criticized (fairly or unfairly)

8. Severs relationships over opinions (Perhaps rather hyperbolic—but you get the picture.)

The textbook illustration for such antagonism is the political rhetoric in nations where "free speech" is allowed. Anger, accusations, and vitriol fly like arrows in a medieval war! It seems that we are in a deplorable contest to decide who can be the most aggressively hateful. Unfortunately, such unscriptural cultural behavior has crept into the church. Coming from the young in Christ/immature believers? Yes, and that has always been and is not surprising. However, even among Spirit-filled saints of many years, brothers/sisters in the faith get their "hackles up" (if you are from the deep South, you understand this expression). Yes, Paul and Barnabas had a contentious dispute over a ministry partner (Acts 15:36–41). Yes, Paul challenged Peter in a public setting (Galatians 2:11–21). Those who wish to justify their own personal behavior cite these examples. It is important to remember that the Bible is truthful—it exposes the humanity/carnality/sinful actions of even the most well-known spiritual leaders. The failure of others does not justify ours!

So how do you "submit [your] strength in a posture of meekness," realizing that even the most devout have intense pressures—both externally from culture (Romans 12:2) and internally from the depraved nature (Galatians 5:16–17)?

1. Be ever sensitive to the Holy Spirit, allowing Him to uncover any/all areas in your life that are not Christlike, carnal or unscriptural.

2. Honestly acknowledge personal shortcomings, and earnestly desire for spiritual change and growth.

3. Do your part while, at the same time, recognizing that true spiritual growth is accomplished only by the working of the Holy Spirit.

4. Do not confuse personal preferences with scriptural absolutes.

5. Rely on the Holy Spirit for wisdom when it becomes necessary to address a sensitive issue.

6. Do not diminish others, who may never agree with your position on nonessential" matters (those not violating scriptural principles).

7. Do not assume a hostile/adversarial attitude toward other believers.

8. In these days of social media, do not engage in debate to prove your point of view/theological position/scriptural interpretation/etc. on Facebook/Instagram/Twitter. Unfortunately, even when a writer has pure motives, they can be quickly misunderstood. Harsh words, attacking the person, are far too frequently the result of such provocative discussions. There are other appropriate forums for such important theological considerations when the matter can be more thoroughly examined.

9. Refrain from speaking quickly ("off the cuff") on every subject. The instruction of the Word is to "be quick to hear, slow to speak" (James 1:19, ESV).

10. Be certain you have the facts. Do not judge a situation on rumors, incomplete information, or supposition.

> If you are not an eyewitness, then you are a false witness!

11. Consider the implications of your words/actions. They have both influence on others and personal consequences.

12. Do not assume the negative. Judging the motives of others is unscriptural (Matthew 7:1–2) and very often leads to erroneous conclusions.

> "A gentle answer turns away wrath, but a harsh word stirs up anger" (Proverbs 15:1, NIV).

> "Let your conversation be always full of grace, seasoned with salt (to be palatable, to preserve), so that you may know how to answer everyone" (Colossians 4:6, NIV, explanations mine).

> "The servant of the Lord must not quarrel, but must be gentle toward all people, able to teach, patient, in gentleness instructing those in opposition" (2 Timothy 2:24–25, MEV).

> "To speak evil of no one, not to be contentious, but gentle, showing all humility toward everyone..." (Titus 3:2, MEV).

> "But the wisdom from above is first of all pure. It is also peace loving, gentle at all times, and willing to yield to others" (James 3:17, NLT).

Spirit-filled believers grow/mature at individual rates. However, in these days of such intense mistrust, frustration, and extremely polarized opinions in almost every sector of society, it is of utmost significance that we all carefully monitor our words/responses. Perhaps the phrase should be elevated to "pray before you speak" rather than "think before you speak."

Be gentle—*then your words will be gentle!*

MY THOUGHTS:

THE WRONG ADJECTIVE?

Adjectives are meant to be descriptive. They provide the "color commentary" (details) for the subject being discussed. (No, this is not an English lesson!) For example, compare the impulsive fisherman Simon Peter with the apostle Peter on the Day of Pentecost or John the "son of thunder" with the beloved apostle John. And sometimes the words seem to take on a life of their own. If a reference is made to the apostle Thomas, it is quite likely that you immediately think of the adjective *doubting*, which is derived from his comments following the resurrection of Christ (John 20:24–29). It tends to paint him in a negative light. But is this really an accurate description of this apostle?

From the biblical text, other than his name being included with the listing of other disciples, he is mentioned only on three specific occasions, all in the Gospel of John and all very significant.

Allow me to challenge your thinking about the events in which Thomas is a central figure. Perhaps other descriptive adjectives more correctly indicate the deep faith of this apostle who (traditionally) carried the gospel to India and was subsequently martyred there.

JOHN 11

The events surrounding the death/restoration to life of Lazarus. As an aside, I purposely did not use the word

77

resurrection, as it indicates a permanent deliverance from/ over death. Jesus was the *"firstfruits of them that slept"* (1 Corinthians 15:23, KJV). At some later date, Lazarus died again; Jesus did not. That is another subject, so let's return to the narrative. When Jesus told His disciples that He was going back to the area near Jerusalem, the disciples strongly protested the wisdom of returning. In the very recent past, the Jewish people there wanted to stone Him. To those devout Jews, Jesus was guilty of blasphemy. He had boldly claimed to be the *"Son of God"* (John 10:22–38). But notice, it was Thomas who said to the other disciples, *"Let us also go, that we may die with him"* (John 11:16, ESV). Other translations clarify even further, *"...die with Jesus"* (NLT).

An adjective to describe Thomas? *Loyally committed.*

Quite likely Thomas did not fully comprehend the motivation of Jesus at that moment. Did this return into a hostile environment seem reasonable/logical to him? Probably not. The point is, Thomas said to the other disciples that this was the time to trust Jesus—even if it meant death. And what about us? The future may be extremely confusing/uncertain. It would be easy to protest any faith-action on the basis on what is "reasonable" to the human intellect. The oft-forgotten chorus seems appropriate here: "I have decided to follow Jesus; no turning back!"

JOHN 14

In the final discourse Jesus had with His disciples prior to the Cross, He is explaining that He will soon leave *"to prepare a place for you"* and *"will come and get you"* (John 14:2–3, NLT). Then Jesus declares, *"You know the way to where I am going"* (v. 4, NLT). The response of Thomas is emphatic. *"No, we don't know, Lord...We have no idea where you are going, so how can we know the way?"* (v. 5, NLT).

An adjective to describe Thomas? *Honestly searching.*

The Lord is not offended by sincere questions. In actuality, He is offended by a "fake faith" that denies reality. It seems rather obvious that the Creator has the ability to answer any question posed by the created!

The Old Testament prophet Habakkuk openly questioned God about the manner in which He was dealing with Judah. When God provided the plan of action—that He would use the Babylonians to punish Judah—the prophet was even more distressed. Finally, the Lord said, "*This vision is for a future time.... If it seems slow in coming, wait patiently, for it will surely take place*" (Habakkuk 2:3, NLT).

Keep on searching the Word. Speak to a loving Father openly and sincerely. He really wants us to know Him personally and live in the confident assurance of His love and grace.

JOHN 20

On the first evening (Sunday night) of the resurrection of Christ, the Lord miraculously appeared to the disciples who were hiding behind locked doors. There were ten disciples in the room. Of course, Judas Iscariot was not there, and for some unknown reason, Thomas was not present. Excitedly the disciples told Thomas, "*We have seen the Lord!*" (John 20:25, NLT). But Thomas was not convinced. Here is where the tag "doubting" is often applied. "*I won't believe it unless I see the nail wounds in his hands, put my fingers into them, and place my hand into the wound in his side*" (v. 25, NLT). "*Eight days later the disciples were together again, and this time Thomas was with them*"! (v. 26). Jesus again appeared miraculously and spoke directly to Thomas. He pointed to His wounds and told Thomas not to be faithless any longer. To which Thomas shouted, "*My Lord and my God!*" (vv. 26–28, NLT).

An adjective to describe Thomas? *Experientially confirming.*

Personally, I do not think that Thomas was debunking the other disciples. He did not question their experience. He just wanted to be absolutely certain that the Christ they described was the same one he had seen so brutally tortured, hanging on the cross only a few days earlier.

It is important to remember that when Mary Magdalene told the disciples of her encounter with Christ, *"they didn't believe her"* (Mark 16:11, NLT). Later, two of His followers met Jesus on the road, and when they returned to Jerusalem *"to tell the others,...no one believed them"* (v. 12, NLT). On another occasion, Jesus appeared to the Eleven and *"rebuked them for their stubborn unbelief because they refused to believe those who had seen him after he had been raised from the dead"* (v. 14, NLT).

> The Christ that we see must have the nail scars in His hands and feet and the scar from the spear in His side.

So, in reality Thomas was no different from the other believers, including the other apostles! This was dramatic. To this point they had not yet comprehended that the Messiah would not bring immediate deliverance from Roman oppression. It took a rather long while for the full intent of His death/burial/resurrection to become a spiritual reality. Incidentally, the last recorded question of the apostles before Jesus ascended into heaven was *"Will you at this time restore the kingdom?"* (Acts 1:6, ESV). My conclusion is a positive one. I think Thomas had the right idea. The Christ he wanted to see/know was the One with the nail-scarred hands and pierced side. And when Thomas had the personal encounter/experience with the risen Savior, the revelation of who He is was dramatic and powerful. *"My Lord and my God!"* (John 20:28). At this moment Thomas ascribed both lordship and deity to Jesus. No other testimony was necessary!

Valuable lessons from Thomas' personal encounter with Christ:

- Thomas was not satisfied with depending on the experience of others.

- Thomas did not want to be deceived by accepting less than factual evidence.

- Thomas was willing to accept only the Christ of the Cross.

- Thomas moved into the realm of spiritual revelation with a public affirmation that Jesus is indeed God.

The Spirit will reveal the resurrected Christ to you, and there is ample reason to shout, "My Lord and my God!"

So, when we investigate a bit deeper into the spiritual development of Thomas, perhaps the adjective doubting does not correctly nor adequately define his growing level of faith. In the future I think I will forego that particular adjective when speaking of this faithful servant of Jesus Christ.

By the way, now that we have the inspired Word of God, there is written record that Jesus Christ is the living Lord and Savior, seated at the heavenly Father's right hand where He faithfully intercedes on our behalf (Hebrews 7:25).

MY THOUGHTS:

Reveal Your Glory

H. M. L.

H. MAURICE LEDNICKY
Arr. by Nate Carter

Re-veal Your glo - ry in me, re - veal Your glo - ry in me
Re-veal Your glo - ry through me, re - veal Your glo - ry through me

As I stand in Your pre - sence___ re - veal Your glo - ry in me;
As I live by Your grace_____ re - veal Your glo - ry through me;

So that I___ may know Your e - ter - nal maj - es - ty.
So that oth - ers may know Your e - ter - nal maj - es - ty.

I now wor - ship You, Lord, re - veal Your glo - ry in me.___
By the pow'r of Your love re - veal Your glo - ry through me.___

82

THE AGNOSTIC EPIDEMIC

Recently I heard a news commentator declare himself as agnostic—then set about to describe the crucifixion of Christ and its purpose for blocking man from God's judgment. (Actually, though not intended as such and using different terminology, it was a pretty good salvation message.)

Let me pause to quote the dictionary definition of an agnostic:

> *"a person who holds the view than any ultimate reality (such as God) is unknown and probably unknowable; one who is committed to not believing in either the existence or nonexistence of God or a god"*

So the agnostic does not really say there is no God, but just that, in his/her mind, there are too many inconsistencies to accept a Supreme Being. In my opinion this is a huge/serious problem in this "enlightened" generation. Even among those who publicly declare their belief in God, a significant contingency would question/reject the idea of a personal, knowable God. The humanistic approach to justice/fairness/equality is squarely juxtaposed against a compassionate/caring/forgiving God. It has been Satan's tactic from his initial lies to Adam/Eve in the Garden of

Eden. "God did not mean what He said—He doesn't want you to know."

REALITY OF GOD

The number one "biggie" in mentally/intellectually questioning the personal reality of God is *if* there is a God, why is there so much injustice in the world? The poverty, famine, wars, disease, disasters—it all seems so unfair for a loving God to allow this.

I realize that the person who wants to argue the matter will go back to "original sin" and predestination and divine foreknowledge and, and, and (subjects for another occasion). What is often omitted is the inescapable truth of man's depravity—the nature no longer pure or innocent but relentlessly bent toward evil. *"There is not righteous, no not one..."* (Romans 3:10). This verse is quoted from Psalm 14:1–3 which strongly declares that man is corrupt. The Hebrew word is even more emphatic and translates as filthy. *"For all have sinned and come short of the glory of God"* (Romans 3:23, KJV). The prophet Isaiah used the diseased leper to illustrate the seriousness of man's sin. *"For we have all become like one who [ceremonially] is unclean [like a leper], and all our deeds of righteousness are like filthy rags; we all wither and decay like a leaf, and our wickedness[our sin, our injustice, our wrongdoing], like the wind, take us away [carrying us far from God's favor, toward destruction]"* (Isaiah 64:6, AMPC). The consequences of human behavior—even impacting those who are righteous—are staggering and grow exponentially from generation to generation. What God intended for His moral creation (angels and humans) was for them to be in fellowship with Him. Hence, man (and angels) were created with a free will—the power to choose. God did not want forced worship!

Yes, we all are distressed by what our world has become—but that was not the Father's plan, nor is it His fault. The Son came to restore man's relationship with a Holy God and will ultimately defeat everyone and everything that is in rebellion. This truth is not the result of human intellect but of/by divine revelation!

GOOD WORKS

Then, pushing for a close second place is the idea of good works in view of a "loving" God who, of course, would never declare judgment upon good people who are sincere. With such a syncretistic mixture of religions (i.e., Eastern mysticism, New Age, pseudo-Christian, etc., etc.), the new (unscriptural) definition of tolerance, and the rejection of any/all absolutes, one is easily allowed to determine what is/is not moral. God is expected to understand and accept our reasoning of right-wrong.

Let's push the envelope a bit further into the ranks of modern Christianity. Common thought embraces the idea that being kind, honest, and loyal to family/friends all move one up the ladder in earning the acceptance and favor of God. A recent study indicated that the majority of Christians believe that if you do certain things, you will have material blessings and also escape the difficulties others encounter. Grace is necessary only if you have really been glaringly evil, for which the consequences of such behavior are self-destructive or serious enough to incur the wrath of God.

All Scripture is divinely inspired; hence, Paul and James do not contradict each other on the matter of works and grace. Incidentally, the letters and epistles were directed to the specific needs of specific audiences and, therefore , did not even attempt to discuss all subject matter. In the books of Romans and Galatians the Apostle Paul provides a prolific apologetic on the singularity of grace for salvation. Perhaps the most concise statement in scripture is Ephesians 2:8–9: "For by grace you have been saved through faith, and this is not of yourselves. It is the gift of God, not of works so that no one should boast" (MEV). James, in my opinion, strengthens, rather than diminishes, the teaching of Paul by clarifying the relational manifestation of the two.

"*So faith by itself, if it has not works, is dead. But a man may say, 'You have faith and I have works'. Show me your faith without your works, and I will show you my faith by my works*" (James 2:17–18, MEV). Both Paul and James us Abraham as an example. One to show that Abraham's faith came before his acceptance of the covenant (through circumcision); the other to show that after his initial faith experience, Abraham obediently responded to offer his son Isaac. In both instances, faith was being expressed through/by works.

MULTIPLE RELIGIONS

Now we come to the idea of multiple religions, all with distinct philosophies; however, many of the followers are people of "faith" (not to be confused with biblical faith) and espouse morality (that also being individually defined). So which is correct? How can anyone really know in this earthly life?

The whole concept of "religious tolerance" has taken on a new meaning in recent years. The "many roads lead to heaven" concept has been around for many years but has taken on new impetus in recent times. So the agnostic is confused. Surely God would not be so narrow minded as to demand that it must be His way or else. The self-righteous mantra becomes, "Jesus may be your truth, but He is not mine." The more the agnostic tries to put it all together intellectually, the less he/she believes about the possibility of fellowship with a personal God.

HYPOCRISY

And, of course, aimed primarily at dedicated followers of Christ is the timeworn, finger- pointing accusation of hypocrisy. To be certain, we are all imperfect, but in a self-justifying mode, the agnostic concludes that such imperfections are systemic rather than individual failures. In short, it is God's fault. So how would it ever be possible to believe in a God whose followers are such poor representatives of His teachings? (Unfortunately, some of the criticism is justified.)

Have you ever heard, "I don't even claim to be a Christian and I wouldn't do that," or "I don't go to church because of all the hypocrites"? Eventually, a loving, forgiving Father is dismissed as either irrelevant to contemporary culture or incapable of having a viable impact on the personal lives of His followers. Over the years I have spoken with scores of young people who have observed a vast chasm between profession and practice and have been turned off to any semblance of organized religion. It goes without saying that many institutions of higher learning have positioned agnostic professors in the classroom, and at every opportunity they plant seeds of doubt about the reality of personal fellowship with a spiritual (invisible to human eye) being.

As this epidemic grows, the whole meaning of the miraculous birth/sinless life/substitutionary death/resurrection of Christ is totally eclipsed by faulty logic and philosophies. Because as humans we find it difficult to grasp concepts without the aid of external senses (see, touch, etc.), the agnostic does not envision the eternal truth that the Savior came into the world to be "one of us." This, in the simplest of terms, is revelation by faith.

> *"Look! The virgin will conceive a child! She will give birth to a son, and they will call him Immanuel, which means 'God is with us'"* (Matthew 1:23, NLT).

> *"And the Word (Jesus) became flesh and dwelt among us, and we have seen his glory, glory as of the only Son from the Father, full of grace and truth"* (John 1:14, ESV).

> *"Though he was God, he did not think of equality with God as something to cling to. Instead, he gave us his divine privileges; he took the humble position of a slave and was born as a human being. When he appeared in human form, he humbled himself in obedience to God and died a criminal's death on a cross"* (Philippians 2:6–8, NLT, addition mine).

Christ's came so that we could have restored fellowship with the Father—the original intent for the creation of man. Yes, I believe in a personal, knowable God. He loves me. And each day offers a glorious reminder of the incredible truth that even though we are marked by the propensity to sin and our own personal sin, the giving of the Son by the Eternal Father and the Son's substitutionary sacrifice provides the exclusive opportunity for redemption, reconciliation, and restoration. Hallelujah!

MY THOUGHTS:

HIS GLORY—OUR BENEFIT

It's a scriptural principle of major significance. We must settle it in our spirit and accept it intellectually—emotions will soon follow in step.

In his second letter to the believers at Thessalonica, the apostle Paul (divinely inspired) expresses this truth both succinctly and clearly.

> "We proudly tell God's other churches about your endurance and faithfulness in all the persecutions and hardships (tribulations, afflictions) you are suffering. And God will use this persecution to show his justice and to make you worthy of his Kingdom, for which you are suffering. In his justice he will pay back those who persecute you" (2 Thessalonians 1:4-6, NLT, emphasis and explanations mine).

If one tries to intellectually (apart from the Spirit) understand/reconcile the inexplicable, he/she will constantly live in the fog of confusion and frustration. It all comes back to knowing that a loving heavenly Father is preparing us for the eternal. This one foundational acceptance of scriptural truth will determine our approach to this earthly journey—joy or sadness, sweetness or bitterness, peace or inner turmoil, self-worth (in Christ) or self-pity, victor or victim!

OK—we get the personal benefit part, but how does this run on a parallel track with God's own glory? Can these two function or even exist simultaneously and have complementary significance? Emphatically, yes!

Initially, the appropriate response is a valiant attempt to put our minds around the awesome *greatness of the Almighty*. Nothing is even difficult for Him (Jeremiah 32:17). That realization nudges us in the right direction. The prophet Isaiah with such beautiful language describes the magnificence of God. "*Who else has held the oceans in his hand? Who has measured off the heavens with his fingers? Who else knows the weight of the earth or has weighed the mountains and hills on a scale? Who is able to advise the Spirit of the Lord? Who knows enough to give him advice or teach him? Has the Lord ever needed anyone's advice? Does he need instruction about what is good? Did someone teach him what is right or show him the path of justice? No, for all the nations of the world are but a drop in the bucket. They are nothing more than dust on the scales. He picks up the whole earth as though it were a grain of sand*" (Isaiah 40:12–15, NLT).

Yet another track must also be in focus. Simply, the *goodness of God*. Throughout Scripture He is depicted as a loving heavenly Father who desires only the very best for His children. Seeing His sons and daughters enduring difficulties while faithfully walking in obedience to His Word confirms eternal purpose. From our submissive trust, the Father receives true glory. Old Testament luminaries, such as Joseph, Moses, David, Daniel, etc., provide undeniable examples of the goodness of God, even when every external appearance shouted exactly the opposite. Remember, they did not know the ultimate outcome. They were willing to trust God and understood His sovereign goodness on their behalf.

I suppose the concept is really not so difficult to accept objectively—it does become exponentially more challenging at the point of subjective involvement. So let this be a word from the Lord for a weary, burdened heart. God really does love you! He really does know and care about your circumstances. *"So then, since we have a great High Priest who has entered heaven, Jesus the Son of God, let us hold firmly to what we believe. This High Priest of ours understands our weaknesses, for he faced all of the same testings we do, yet he did not sin. So let us come boldly to the throne of our gracious God. There we will receive his <u>mercy</u>, and we will find <u>grace</u> to help us when we need it most"* (Hebrews 4:14–16, NLT, emphasis mine). *"But because Jesus lives forever, his priesthood lasts forever. Therefore he is able, <u>once and forever</u>, to save those who come to God through him. He lives <u>forever to intercede with God on their behalf</u>"* (Hebrews 7:24–25, NLT, emphasis mine). That surely emphasizes God's intentions for His children.

In spite of every appearance, on the other side of the deep valley, the ultimate outcome (which may or may not be our desire/preference) will further develop the image of Christ within. It is one more step toward the indescribable moment of eternal graduation into the Father's house. *"For our present troubles are small and won't last very long. Yet they produce for us a glory that vastly outweighs them and will last forever! So we don't look at the troubles we can see now; rather, we fix our gaze on things that cannot be seen. <u>For the things we see now will soon be gone, but the things we cannot see will last forever</u>"* (2 Corinthians 4:17–18, NLT, emphasis mine).

Today with clear minds, honest hearts, and courageous faith, let's remind ourselves: this moment/season is but another chapter in this brief earthly journey that will accrue to my personal spiritual benefit, and in it/through it God will receive glory!

> *"Now may the God of peace—who brought up from the dead our Lord Jesus, the great Shepherd of the sheep, and ratified an eternal covenant with his blood—may he equip you will all you need for*

doing his will. May he produce in you, through the power of Jesus Christ, every good thing that is pleasing to him. All glory to him forever and ever! Amen" (Hebrews 13:20–21, NLT).

MY THOUGHTS:

TEN BARRIERS TO IMMORAL BEHAVIOR

Driving home one afternoon, the Scripture *"Died Abner as a fool dieth?"* just popped into my mind. It apparently came out of nowhere. If you rehearse the story for a moment (2 Samuel 3), you recall that after King Saul died and David became king in Judah, Abner, who was King Saul's general, continued to wage war against David. Finally, after approximately seven years, Abner met with David and agreed to support him as king over the entire nation. However, when Joab (one of David's military leaders) heard this, he was furious, as Abner had killed his younger brother. In a pretense of wanting to talk with General Abner, Joab called him aside and killed him. King David was distraught. He immediately declared that he was unaware of this and had not sanctioned this terrible murder. As David followed the funeral procession, he uttered the statement, *"Died Abner as a fool dieth?"* His point was that this mighty general had not been defeated; rather, he had been deceived.

With that thought playing in my mind, I went to the office and began to ask the Lord the reason for this unusual experience. As I meditated, the Lord spoke to my heart about the deception of immorality.

Within a few days I preached a sermon from this passage. Later, I discovered that a well-known, respected minister was in the audience that morning. A short time later he was caught in the very act of an adulterous relationship. He had not surreptitiously preplanned to violate his commitment to his wife and to the Lord—but he had been deceived by Satan himself. What a horrible price he paid for this deception. Only a few minutes of occasional "pleasure" brought personal shame and regret for a lifetime. Of course, God is merciful and forgiving when there is repentance; however, His written Word speaks explicitly to the divine plan that offers specific instruction as to how the destructive pitfalls of immoral behavior can be avoided.

So, I have distilled in very simple terms ten rather obvious, but extremely important, barriers to immoral behavior.

1. Conviction of the Holy Spirit (This should immediately stop any further movement that could ultimately lead to sexual immorality!)

2. Personal relationship with Christ

3. Sacredness of marriage vows

4. Love for your spouse

5. Love for your children and family

6. Respect for the Body of Christ (the church)

7. Damage to personal testimony among believers/ unbelievers

8. Serious consequences to spiritual purity

9. Emotional effects on your spouse, children, and other people

10. Possibility of negative physical consequences (i.e., pregnancy, disease, etc.)

The simple truth is that God established the guidelines for sexual purity: one man married to one woman for life. Any and all sexual involvement between two persons who are not married to each other is sinful. It may be offensive to some; however, I am personally convinced that viewing explicitly pornographic materials is categorically the same, in the eyes of a holy God, as the physical act of fornication or adultery. In the Sermon on the Mount, Jesus spoke these pungent words:

> The God-given desire for physical relationship must be disciplined and controlled according to Scripture.

"You have heard the commandment that says, 'You must not commit adultery.' But I say, anyone who <u>even looks at a woman with lust has already committed adultery with her in his heart</u>. So, if your eye—even your good eye—causes you to lust, gouge it out and throw it away" (Matthew 5:27–30, NLT, emphasis mine).

Often I have been asked, "Why is this such a universal temptation?" The answer is clear from Scripture. In the sacred confines of marriage, loving sexual expression is sanctioned and approved by God. The monogamous relationship of one man with one woman was the very first covenant that God ordained (Genesis 2:24). Outside of marriage the opposite is true. God strongly condemns such behavior (Exodus 20:14; Matthew 19:4–6, 9). In other words, God created men and women to enjoy the physical relationship. So, because God Himself instilled this physical attraction in His creation, it is not a sin *unless* an individual chooses to bypass the sacred plan of God.

The desire is not the problem—rather, violating the plan and purpose of the Creator creates numerous problems and painful consequences.

> *This wonderful plan of God is not restrictive; it is both liberating and protective. Brothers and sisters, guard yourselves very carefully. Don't ever even take the first step toward immoral behavior!*

95

IMMATURITY

The Bible clearly teaches that spiritual maturation is vital for the followers of Christ and is a long-term, progressive growth process. Jesus informed Nicodemus, "You _must_ be born again" (John 3:7, emphasis mine). Paul instructed the believers at Ephesus to "_grow up into him_" (Ephesians 4:15, KJV). In the NLT the wording of verses 13–14 emphasizes maturity in Christ: "_until we all come to such unity in our faith and knowledge of God's Son that we will be mature in the Lord...Then we will no longer be immature like children_" (emphasis mine). In view of the Lord's soon return, Peter urged believers to "_grow in the grace and knowledge of our Lord and Savior Jesus Christ_" (2 Peter 3:18, emphasis mine).

In theological jargon the terms _justification_ and _sanctification_ are employed in defining this process. Justification (the formal acquittal of sin) occurs at the precise moment of a revelatory encounter (repentance of sin, faith in the efficacy of the Cross) with the living Savior. This is instantaneous holiness. Now, through Christ, we have access to the Father and begin to live in divine grace (Romans 8:1–2). However, at this moment the sanctification process only begins. It can be described as a commencement, not a completion. The inner work of the Holy Spirit nudges us forward in developing the image of Christ in our lives.

However, we do not simply occupy a chair and wait for it to happen. The Spirit points the way, and we follow His guidance. By the way, the Spirit and the Word are never in conflict or competition as to God's plan and purpose. It is here that the human will comes into sharp focus. Bluntly stated, the Spirit will not force obedient submission. It is my personal choice. And herein begins the discussion relating to spiritual maturity.

1. **Immaturity of the individual is not a systemic problem that implies divine imperfections.** If the principles of scriptural truth are not personally actualized, it does not mean the eternal plan is somehow flawed, inadequate, or irrelevant. Criticisms against Christianity are misplaced. However, the unbeliever often takes aim at individuals who fail to obediently walk in the steps of the Master, employing them as justification for not becoming a follower of Christ. It is equally devastating for a believer to blame God when life's circumstances do not proceed in the direction he/she desires. True, we may not always understand and perhaps even ask why. However, there is a major distinction between asking and accusing.

2. **Immaturity must be recognized for what it is.** Spiritual immaturity and doctrinal extremism are not synonymous. One is the product of an unwillingness to respond appropriately; the other is an aggressive overreach. The tragedy of any church culture that measures itself by itself is enormous. Jesus confronted this issue in the Sermon on the Mount (Matthew 5–7). *"You have heard...but I say"* significantly elevated the priority of inner holiness. Conformity to a doctrinal creed does not necessarily imply spiritual maturity. Some of the most pious people can be seriously unsanctified. Refer to our Lord's incisive comments/condemnation of the Pharisees, Sadducees, scribes, and teachers of the Law.

3. **Immaturity should never be considered a permanent destination.** Because of their immature faith, the children of Israel spent forty years wandering in the wilderness when it was only an eleven-day journey from Mt. Sinai to Kadesh

Barnea (the crossing of the Jordan River into the Promised Land) (Deuteronomy 1:2). They had faith to leave Egypt but not enough to enter the giant-infested Canaan! Emotional pains of past events can be healed by the grace of God. Attitudes and actions based on a personal relationship with Christ will steadily replace reactionary living. Mountains too high to cross eventually become small anthills to step over. The number of years as a believer no more guarantees spiritual maturity than chronological age guarantees wisdom. Unfortunately, we all know people in both categories, spiritual and natural, whose behavior frequently exhibits some very immature characteristics.

4. Immaturity gives rises to extremes in practice. I have lived enough years to know there have been numerous extremes in Pentecostal circles. Following the latest trends without considering the scriptural implications/principles or long-term impact on the body of Christ is often the result of not being grounded in the Word. This is not peculiar to the twenty-first century! It was happening in the early New Testament church. Remember that both Jew and Gentile were just coming into the salvation experience through the provision of Jesus Christ. They did not have the written New Testament. From the demands of the Jewish believers that everyone be circumcised to the misuse of spiritual gifts among the Gentiles, confusion and division were frequent characteristics of the infant church. Paul, Peter, John, Jude, and James (authors of the New Testament following the Gospels and Acts) all warned about extremes in the church.

> The church of Jesus Christ is deeply wounded by those who spend more time in fault-finding than in personal soul-searching.

5. Immaturity often leads to a harsh, judgmental spirit toward others (both believer and unbelievers) whose personal lives do not conform to the nonnegotiables of Scripture and/or one's personal level of commitment. It is the mote-beam issue that Jesus spoke about (Matthew 7:3–5). Sitting on the seat of judgment is a high, holy place reserved for the Almighty! Any attitude of spiritual elitism is "red-flag" evidence of spiritual immaturity.

The reality is that there are no perfect individuals. If we are focused on the *"prize of the high calling of God in Christ Jesus"* (Philippians 3:14, KJV), there will be little time to search out the shortcomings of others. The focused attention of our peripheral vision should be on the secret, deceptive attacks of Satan, whose nefarious desire is to bring shame to our Lord and His church.

Years ago, as a very young pastor (in my early twenties), I often visited a lady whose husband had abandoned her when their baby was born with serious birth defects. The son was my age but had never developed beyond an infant. Although he had grown physically, she had to feed him, change his diapers, and care for him as for a baby of only a few weeks old. Very seldom could she attend church because of her responsibility with her son, but I learned several lessons from that experience. First of all, she was never critical of her former husband. She did not feel sorry for herself but was constantly thanking God for His blessings and grace. As a means of livelihood, she ironed clothes (way back before no-iron clothes were available). Each time I stopped by her very small rental house, I went away with deep gratitude for God's amazing grace to sustain even in the most difficult of circumstances. But I also pondered the significance of spiritual growth and development by this very heartrending example of the failure to develop physically and mentally. It is the divine plan that everyone should grow in Christ and not continue to live as spiritual infants. Through the daily nourishment of the inspired Word of God, with a balanced diet of truth, strong men and women are consistently maturing. While each individual uniquely grows, his/her life should be an obvious testimony to the glorious God of mercy and grace!

HOW DO I KNOW THAT I AM MATURING?

When I reach the level that I do not always have to be the

one on the receiving end of the blessing—I have a heart felt desire to serve. Mature saints joyfully give of themselves to others.

Holy Spirit, teach us, correct us, guide us to become a reflection of Jesus Christ.

MY THOUGHTS:

IN ONE DOOR...OUT THE OTHER!

The Old Testament prophet Ezekiel (a young priest who had been taken captive to Babylon) was a man of "visions" (plural) that came directly from the sovereign Lord. He spoke only as the Lord directed, primarily to the horrific sins of Israel but also to the coming judgment of God on surrounding nations. Sixty-two times, Ezekiel repeats the statement *"They shall know that I am the Lord."* As with the message of many Old Testament prophets, the Almighty offers hope and restoration through the voice of Ezekiel if/when there is true heart repentance. Consequently, the last one-third of the book relates to the future restoration of the nation of Israel. Specifically, the final nine chapters (Ezekiel 40–48) address the glory of the restored Temple during Christ's reign on earth. In the truest definition of a prophet, Ezekiel was both *forth telling* (current circumstances) and *foretelling* (future events).

The verse that intrigued me in a recent study:

> *"But when the people come in through the north gateway to worship the Lord...they must leave by the south gateway. And those who entered through the south gateway must leave by the north gateway. They must never leave by the same gateway they came in, but must always use the opposite gateway"* (Ezekiel 46:9, NLT, emphasis mine).

Indeed, a strange instruction. The worshipers were to enter one door and exit on the opposite end of the Temple. The exact reason for this instruction could only be speculation; however, several thoughts could be possibilities for consideration.

1. **This would provide for an orderly flow of the "coming-going" of the worshipers.** Surely, we serve a God who is very disciplined and orderly. Just consider the precise nature of every aspect of the creation, to say nothing of the human body which is *"fearfully and wonderfully made"* (Psalm 139:14). The incredible advances in scientific studies about the universe should cause us to shout with an even louder voice than David the songwriting shepherd: *"When I consider your heavens...which you have set in place..."* (Psalm 8:3, NIV, emphasis mine). There are estimates of 40–50 billion stars in the Milky Way (the galaxy in which the earth is positioned), and according to the Psalmist, *"He counts the number of the stars; He calls them all by their names"* (Psalm 147:4, MEV, emphasis mine; also see Isaiah 40:26).

2. **Perhaps, in some manner, the intention was to maintain a sacred decorum in His holy house.** As an aside (personally), I have to strain a bit to connect the casual attitude in His house (i.e., eating, drinking in the sanctuary during worship music/preaching of the Word) with the holiness of the Sovereign, Creator, Redeemer. If absolute holiness is a divine attribute of the Almighty (Isaiah 6:1–3) and worship is a primary function of the believer (Psalm 96:8–9), the two must be inextricably joined in the deepest of humility and reverence. To come into the house of worship in a cavalier or preoccupied manner will quite likely result in "leaving the same way we came in" or perhaps even worse spiritually. Is it possible that our informality in God's house has somewhat dulled our senses to the sacred privilege of being in the presence of the eternal sovereign God? This is not about liturgy or restricting the flow of the Holy Spirit. *Reverence is basic to receiving.* All through scriptural record the clear picture is that men/women fell on their faces

when they recognized the presence of the Almighty. OK, OK, I'm moving right along...

3. The most striking explanation is perhaps the simplest. The symbolism is readily understood. It has nothing to do with a passageway for entrance or egress. **Never leave the Lord's house the same way you entered.** That speaks to individuals at every level of spiritual maturity and to every type of human need. It requires a mind-set of faith—expecting that you will personally meet with the Father/Son/Holy Spirit and the blessed Trinity will supernaturally interact with your spirit, mind, and body. Having been witness to some of the earlier days of tent revivals and personally seeing many outstanding miracles, one thing was obvious—the people who desired supernatural intervention/healing/deliverance from the Lord came with a heightened expectation. (Of course, there were some excesses, but those were the actions of humans desiring to claim God's glory or selfish exploitation. In spite of this, God's power is not abated, and He still honors true faith.)

> God is indeed my friend, but I am certainly not His equal!!

It is only by incomprehensible grace that we can enter His holy presence. And that only through the sacrifice of His Son to redeem us from the Adamic (sinful) nature.

- Every hymn, song, or chorus should be about Him/honoring Him/glorifying Him.

- Every sermon from the Word should penetrate my heart and when applied by the Holy Spirit should guide me to change, resulting in an ever-increasing dimension of Christ-likeness.

- Every prayer should with humility acknowledge His sovereign authority in my life, as well as in the entire course of human history.

It is as basic as believing "I have a need; He has the answer!"

The very next time you enter the Lord's house…Go in reverently and expectantly so that by His love, power, and grace you will go out with joy and peace.

You will come in one way—and go out another!

MY THOUGHTS:

THE GRACE OF HUMILITY: DIFFICULT TO ACHIEVE AND MAINTAIN

As dedicated followers of Christ, we often face a greater temptation from recognition than from rejection. The Word of God says it succinctly: *"A person is tested by being praised"* (Proverbs 27:21, NLT).

- "Success" at any level is difficult to keep in perspective!

- Our strengths are often a prime target for Satan's attacks. We know our weaknesses and guard them carefully. However, our guard is often slack in areas where we seem to be strong.

- Counterfeit holiness is exposed by its lack of humility!

- The inner secret of motivation (known only to the individual), not public behavior, defines the reality/purity of humility.

Check this out...written back in the seventeenth century by Jeremy Taylor (and paraphrased here).

GRACE OF HUMILITY

The grace of humility is exercised in the following rules.

1. Do not think better of yourself because of any outward circumstance that happens to you.

2. Humility does not consist in criticizing yourself, or wearing ragged clothes, or walking around submissively wherever you go. Humility consists in a realistic opinion of yourself, namely, that you are an unworthy person.

3. When you hold this opinion of yourself, be content that others think the same of you.

4. Nurture a love to do good things in secret,…and therefore not highly esteemed because of them. Be content to go without praise.

5. Never be ashamed of your birth or your parents, your occupation or the lowly status of any of them.

6. Never say anything, directly or indirectly, that will provoke praise or elicit compliments from others.

7. When you do receive praise for something you have done, take it indifferently and return it to God.

8. Make a good name for yourself by being a person of virtue and humility.

9. Do not take pride in any praise given to you. Rejoice in God who gives gifts others can see in you.

10. Do not ask others your faults with the intent or purpose being to have others tell you of your good qualities.

11. When you are slighted by someone, or feel undervalued, do not harbor any secret anger.… Do not try to seek out a group of flatterers who will take your side.

12. Do not entertain any of the devil's whispers of pride.

13. Take an active part in the praising of others.

14. Be content when you see or hear that others are doing well in their jobs and with their income, even when you are not.

15. Never compare yourself with others unless it be to advance your impression of them and lower your impression of yourself.

16. Do not constantly try to excuse all of your mistakes…, for virtue scorns a lie for its cover.

17. Give God thanks for every weakness, fault, and imperfection you have. Accept it as a favor of God, an instrument to resist pride and nurse humility.

18. Do not expose others' weakness in order to make them feel less able than you.

19. Remember that what is most important to God is that we submit ourselves and all that we have to Him.[1]

Jeremy Taylor (1613–1667) from
The Rule and Exercises of Holy Living

"Yea, all of you be subject one to another, and be clothed with humility: for God resisteth the proud, and giveth grace to the humble. Humble yourselves therefore under the mighty hand of God, that he may exalt you in due time" (1 Peter 5:5–6, KJV, emphasis mine).

The New Testament Greek word for humility literally means "low-hanging." It is always used in a positive manner, implying "lowliness of mind." The same connotation is employed in Philippians 2, when Paul instructs believers to be lowly in mind (v. 3) and then very explicitly describes the mind of Christ and how it ultimately led Him in humility to a criminal's death on a Roman cross (vv. 5–11).

Andrew Murray (1828–1917), the South African pastor, penned more than fifty books including *Humility*, which has challenged believers all around the world. Though Murray has been dead more than one hundred years, his call to humility is equally (if not more) relevant to this generation than when it was first published. Here are a few quotes to bring sober thought to this important scriptural subject.

> *"The root of all virtue and grace, of all faith and acceptable worship, is that we know that we have nothing but what we receive, and bow in deepest humility to wait upon God for it."*

> *"The holiest will ever be the humblest."*

> *"Humility, the place of entire dependence on God, is...the first duty and the highest virtue of the creature, and the root of every virtue. And so pride, or the loss of this humility, is the root of every sin and evil."*

> *"Humility before God is nothing if not proved in humility before men."*

> *"Humility is nothing but the disappearance of self in the vision that God is all."*[2]

Endnotes

1   Richard J. Foster and James Bryan Smith, ed., *Devotional Classics: Selected Readings for Individuals and Groups, rev. ed.* (San Francisco: HarperSanFrancisco, 2005), 244–248, https://books.google.com/books/about/Devotional_Classics_Revised_Edition.html?id=PviNvknLPO8C.

2   Andrew Murray, *Humility: The Beauty of Holiness* (New York: Fleming H. Revell; Project Gutenberg, 2018), http://www.gutenberg.org/cache/epub/57121/pg57121-images.html.

THE PENTECOSTAL MARRIAGE OF EXPERIENCE AND ENERGY

A personal story to begin: Back in the late 1960s–early 1970s, as a young preacher (in the under-thirty crowd) I was privileged to serve as a district youth leader (aka DCAP). During this tenure, I was invited to minister at the spiritual emphasis week at Southwestern AG University (then Southwestern Bible College). In the middle of that week, I received a call from Elder A. C. Bates asking if we could have lunch together. A word about Brother Bates: He was an esteemed leader in the early days of the Assemblies of God. Actually, he was the first Assemblies of God District Superintendent of the Texaco District, comprised of two states, Texas and New Mexico. (Today, there are four Assemblies of God districts plus Hispanic districts in this same geographical area.) If you recall the name Elder A. C. Bates, you have been around the Assemblies of God for a very long time or are a serious student of early Pentecostal history in Texas. I mention this to emphasize the huge disparity in our ages and experience. He was nearing eighty; I was nearing thirty!

At lunch he posed a question about a portion of Peter's sermon of the Day of Pentecost: "*What does it mean when it says that 'old men will dream dreams' and 'your young men will see visions'?*" (Acts 2:17). He emphatically stated that he did not want to just sit in a rocking chair, simply reminiscing about the past and how things used to be. Even though the time with Elder Bates was delightful and we had a long discussion, I am certain I did not answer his question to either his or my satisfaction.

The "dreams" of the older leaders speak of wisdom gained through experience. The "visions" of the younger leaders confirm the energized zeal and passion to accomplish the mission of the church.

Now that it is my turn to objectively evaluate a long road of ministry, I have been rehearsing this very same passage in my mind. What does this verse really mean? So one day while meditating, I believe the Lord gave me an answer.

At least it satisfied my understanding.

And it was on the Day of Pentecost that this was prophetically declared and soon became clearly evident in the advancing ministry of the early New Testament church.

To be certain, there is no dichotomy of purpose from generation to generation. Each member in Christ's body is to be enriched by what the other members have to offer (1 Corinthians 12:12–27).

Simply said, hopefully without coming across as battling a giant case of self-pity or being egotistical, I know that I no longer have the physical stamina and energy of a Spirit-empowered thirty- or forty-year-old. But by the mercy of people and the grace of God, I have learned a few significant lessons along the journey of faith that may be of help to the younger, aggressive spiritual leaders of the twenty-first century.

Spirit-filled believers are not segregated by age; they are united by the indwelling Holy Spirit.

To assume that chronological years of leadership imply a reservoir of wisdom that is not being accepted, or at least evaluated, by those who are younger or have less experience will most likely result in conflict and confusion in the church. However, the reverse is also true. For the younger leadership to assume that all that has been accomplished for the kingdom by a previous generation is irrelevant to present and future kingdom endeavors can be equally devastating.

The elders must be kind and supportive of the zeal and passion of the younger. The younger must be respectful and appreciative of the many sacrifices made by the elders in preparing the soil, planting, and watering—bringing us to a bountiful harvest in the end time.

Every platform on which I have been privileged to minister was visible evidence of the dedication and commitment of a previous generation to fulfill the Great Commission. The chorus of one of my favorite older hymns, "The Songs of the Reaper," says (in part), "But the tears of the sower and songs of the reaper shall mingle together in joy by and by."

The challenge for every generation is to be able to properly segregate *scriptural principle* from *personal preference*.

Let it here be stated without equivocation that the Word of God does not change from generation to generation. It is absolute truth and must be carefully and explicitly obeyed regardless of cultural mores or geographical location. That is never easy for any age group in the church. Why? The elders have formed some rather strong opinions based on many years of personal and corporate experience. They have witnessed both the good and the bad. Years have given them the advantage of evaluating certain practices. Some they hold closely; others they have discarded as ineffective or irrelevant. The younger, thus far, have significantly less diversity in their experience. This is not in and of itself bad, but it does not bode well to assume that others have done little or nothing or fail to capture the vision of what should be done.

> Idealism is a marvelous trait, but looking reality squarely in the eye will challenge our faith and teach us to more fully extract scriptural principles from generational preferences.

So, to each group his/her experience seems to be the correct way. It is at this point that danger is lurking. IF my conclusions are the only "right way," then I quickly become judgmental and critical of others who do not share my preferences. Preferences have now replaced biblical principles. The obvious conclusion: those who choose to disagree with the "way I do it" are simply wrong. Godly behavior forbids such finger-pointing and attitudes of elitism.

Many years ago, the Lord taught me (in a rather dramatic fashion) that specific styles of leadership must never be the basis for fellowship among true believers. The Holy Spirit brings us together in united purpose—lifting up the name of Jesus to each other and to those who do not yet know His love and grace.

Elders, let's reach out a hand to encourage those who are following in the path we have cleared. Together with them, we will see a release of Pentecostal power and scriptural authority that will impact this end-time generation dramatically.

Young men/women, seek to learn from the heart of those who have sacrificed to provide a platform on which you can stand and advance the kingdom in ever-increasing ways. The ultimate goal is to give all glory and honor to Jesus Christ, Lord and Savior.

> Never be a part of any group that brings confusion and division in the body of Christ based on personal preferences.

On the "birthday" (Day of Pentecost) of the New Testament church, there was prophetic confirmation that *experience* (dreams) and *energy* (visions) must be inextricably joined in Spirit-anointed and empowered ministry. It must never become "us" and "them" in His church. Jesus prayed, "*I pray that they will all be one, just as you and I are one—as you are in me, Father, and I am in you. And may they be in us so that the world will believe you sent me*" (John 17:21, NLT).

THREE STORIES, FOUR WORDS, ONE GLORIOUS TRUTH

The following three events recorded by the Gospel writers appear to have little commonality. Each individually, when studied in its context, offers ample truth to stand alone. Any casual student of the inspired Word can recite these pungent moments in rather specific detail. Yet, in a unique manner, they are inextricably bound together to capture a glorious truth that is foundational to both the faith and fabric of the believer's relationship with the Father Redeemer.

Let's assume a different perspective from the generally accepted core insights revealed by these literal events. Of course, the natural path is to examine these stories in the chronological sequence of scriptural history. This we will do. To step into this particular spiritual arena, it is incumbent that we latch onto the four words that literally define the essence of truth from which the four cornerstones produce a level flooring upon which we all must stand. They are the baseline of unity and purpose.

FOUR KEY WORDS IN EACH PASSAGE:
TOOK, BLESSED, BROKE, GAVE

1. **Feeding the five thousand men plus women/children with five loaves, two fish** (Matthew 14:15–21)

As unique as the information written in John's Gospel is, he was divinely inspired to record this breathtaking event, along with the authors of the Synoptics. It was such a profound miracle that it was retold in all four Gospels! (Speaking of miracles, did you ever wonder how the young boy that Andrew found still had his lunch in hand?!)

The Miracle Of Multiplication: Jesus took the lad's lunch; Jesus blessed the bread and fish. But it was only in the breaking that the miracle of multiplication occurred. It was precisely at this moment that the entire multitude was generously fed.

The application is glaringly obvious! Jesus takes us—as small/insignificant/insufficient/unworthy as we may be.

Then Jesus blesses us—we are made to sit in heavenly places in Christ Jesus (Ephesians 2:6).

But before the Lord can give us, He must break us. Only by being broken can He use us to the fullest potential! Watchman Nee (1903–1972), the Chinese church leader/teacher, declared, "God's basic work is to reduce us."[1] J. R. Miller (1840–1912), a Presbyterian pastor, proclaimed, "Whole, unbruised, unbroken men are of but little use."[2]

2. Final night of the Lord's earthly life: instituting the Lord's Supper (Matthew 26:26–29)

As we often repeat directly from Scripture at Communion, those same four words come leaping forth to provide somber reflection of our Lord's holy mission to fallen man. That powerful example speaks of our present relationship with Christ and encourages us to remember His death in anticipation of His return.

The Mandate Of Suffering/Sacrifice: Without our Lord's suffering/brokenness, we have no possibility of redemption/forgiveness of sin! The graphic prophetic expression of Isaiah 53 can be viewed only with deep introspection. The New Testament authors who had been so very close to Jesus no doubt relived those moments countless times on their own paths of sacrifice/suffering.

Suffering is not a common topic. In fact, our preference is to avoid discussing the correlation between service for Christ and suffering for Christ. But the two are inextricably linked. Paul admonished his son in the faith, Timothy, "*If we suffer, we shall also reign with him*" (2 Timothy 2:12, KJV). In his scholarly apologetic on salvation by faith to the Roman believers, the apostle Paul summarily included the fact of suffering. "*But if we are to share his glory, we must also share his suffering. Yet what we suffer now is nothing compared to the glory he will reveal to us later*" (Romans 8:17–18, NLT, emphasis mine). Obviously, the suffering here relates to our witness for Christ. That is different from the vicissitudes of daily life that cause us pain from time to time. This is not to diminish the intensity of such suffering, just to note that it is not one and the same as being persecuted for Christ's sake. Remember, all of the apostles except John the Beloved were executed for their faith. James was put to death by Herod (Acts 12:2); Peter (2 Peter 1:13–15) and Paul (2 Timothy 4:6–8) spoke openly of their coming executions. Stephen, an early church deacon, was stoned by a mob of angry Jews (Acts 7:54–60).

Not wanting to sound pessimistic or like a calamity howler, yet being realistic of the impending end-time pressure by Satan, I would offer a warning to not be surprised by even more frontal attacks against those who boldly, unashamedly stand for Christ. The evil one does not want to relinquish one inch of territory or one redeemable person. Jesus promised to build His church at the very "gates of hell" (Matthew 16:18).

3. After the resurrection: Christ meeting the two on the road to emmaus and sitting to eat with them (Luke 24:13–31)

As these confused followers of Christ walked with Him that evening, He spoke of prophetic Scriptures. Even then, they did not recognize Him. But as they sat down to eat with Him, they recognized Christ. What opened their eyes? The resurrected Christ repeated those same four words!

The Magnitude Of The Conquest: Now their spiritual eyes were opened; they could put it all together. The ultimate consequence of man's sin had been defeated by Christ's resurrection. Finally, the fear of death had been overcome!

Tie it all together. The three stories point to one glorious truth: the redemptive plan from salvation to eternal victory.

- *Multiplication* for the purpose of personal blessing and the privilege of being a blessing to others

- *Mandate* that requires walking down the pathway of suffering/sacrifice—death to self/carnality for His eternal purpose

- *Magnitude* of joining with our Great Redeemer in resurrected conquest. Finally and for all eternity, the destructive forces of the evil one will be banished from earth and heaven.

Just four simple words—*took, blessed, broke, gave*—repeated in three well-known Bible events, all pointing to one grand and glorious truth!

Endnotes

1   Watchman Nee, *The Glorious Church*, 2nd ed. (Anaheim, CA: Living Stream Ministry, 1993), 133.

2   J. R. Miller, *Making the Most of Life* (New York: Thomas Y. Crowell, 1891), 1, https://books.google.com/books/about/Making_the_Most_of_Life.html?id=7sUVAAAAYAAJ.

MY THOUGHTS:

BIBLICAL MEDICINE

A DOUBLE DOSE OF REALITY

From time to time during my early childhood years, if we became ill, my mother would often prescribe castor oil. If you have never had the privilege of indulging in this medicine (using the term loosely), it has a horrible odor and tastes about like 30 weight motor oil. Suffice it to say, it is very BAD! Yet I have to admit, somewhat begrudgingly, that it usually did work its intended purpose.

Sometimes in life we all need some strong medicine to be brought back to reality. The Bible, so honest that it reveals both the good and the ugly, points to our need for squarely facing the reality of life.

REALITY 1. REALIZING THAT WE ARE LOST AND DOOMED FOR ETERNAL DAMNATION WITHOUT GOD'S GRACE

The horrid truth of human depravity often escapes our conversations, but its reality does not. Illness, behavioral disorders, and other such excusing terms are often used to define the most heinous of evil. The popular book of some years back (by Thomas A. Harris) boldly proclaimed I'm OK—You're

> Scriptural truth is that no one can be found (redeemed, saved) until they realize they are lost!

OK. It may sound good, but it is simply not true. Why is this thinking such a deceitful trick of Satan?

The father of lies (Satan, John 8:44) is still saying, "*God knows that your eyes will be opened as soon as you eat it, and you will be like God, knowing both good and evil*" (Genesis 3:5, NLT, emphasis mine). The consequences of sin are not only personal and time related, but they also extend into the eternal. Without the unmerited favor (mercy and grace) of a loving Father who initiated the one and only path to right relationship with Him—through the sacrifice of His Son, Jesus Christ—we are spiritually and morally destitute. Most know the Scriptures that explicitly define the divine promise—John 3:16; Romans 3:23, 6:23; Ephesians 2:8–9; and many others. But a frequent reminder of this hope sharpens our focus on this glorious salvation with deep gratitude and thanksgiving.

> Never, ever stray away from John 3:16–19.

Nothing, absolutely nothing, that I could ever think, say, or do would pay my sin debt. We are empty handed sitting at the negotiating table with the Eternal Sovereign. This is about as real as it gets!

REALITY 2. UNDERSTANDING THAT SANCTIFICATION IS ALWAYS THE PRE-DICTABLE RESULT OF SAVING GRACE

Today much is being taught/discussed about God's grace. Let it be clearly understood that we can under no circumstance earn His grace. And none of us will ever achieve absolute perfection in this earthly body (see Galatians 5:16–18; 1 John 1:8–10). However, God's grace has been extended not only for our salvation but also for our sanctification.

> A good working definition of sanctification: separated from sin and separated unto God.

One without the other is incomplete. The "fruit" of the Spirit (Galatians 5:22–25) depicts a changed life. Although one is ill advised to judge another—only the Almighty has that assignment—it is scripturally correct to say that the truly born-again believer does not feel comfortable with continuous participation in the actions and attitudes of the unregenerate. *"Do not be unequally yoked with unbelievers. For what partnership has righteousness with lawlessness? Or what fellowship has light with darkness? What accord has Christ with Belial* [Satan]*? Or what portion does a believer share with an unbeliever?... Therefore go out from their midst, and be separate from them, says the Lord"* (2 Corinthians 6:14–15, 17, ESV, emphasis mine).

The reality is that if you are abiding in Christ, you have been transformed from the kingdom of darkness into the kingdom of light (Colossians 1:13–14). Redeemed sons and daughters have a new identity and thus a new desire and loyalty (Philippians 3:8–14). Today you should be more like Christ than you were six months or a year ago. *"Grow in the grace and knowledge of our Lord and Savior Jesus Christ"* (2 Peter 3:18, ESV, Peter's last words). That is reality!

REALITY 3. ACKNOWLEDGING PERSONALLY AND PUBLICLY THAT WE ARE RESPONSIBLE FOR OUR OWN BEHAVIOR

Dare I go here? From Adam and Eve (Genesis 3) to King Saul (1 Samuel 15) to numerous other well-known historical examples, the easiest path to self-justification is to blame some other person or circumstance for destructive, evil behavior. At times, methinks that some politicians have perfected this "art" and could teach a graduate-level course on the subject! Recently I heard that a judge released a criminal who almost beat another man to death in the process of a robbery. His reasoning? The man (far beyond his teen years) did not have parents who taught him to be a good person. Parents often defend their children before an authority (school, etc.) even when they know the child's behavior is not acceptable. Someone else is always to blame. Is it any wonder that prisons are overcrowded and people are afraid to be out at night in certain locations? But these illustrations are the consequences. The real problem is more inward than outward. Remember, out of the heart come the issues of life (Matthew 15:18–19).

It is most refreshing and quickly evokes compassion and a willingness to forgive the person who acknowledges mistakes and wrongdoing without any caveats. Perhaps it may be possible for a person to go through much of this life with excuse after excuse for wrong behavior. But the reality is there is one place it will stop—before the throne of God. The Scripture is clear: everyone will personally give account of himself/herself before God (Romans 14:12).

> Denying to self that he/she is personally responsible for who they are and what they have become is a matter of the heart.

REALITY 4. Refusing to condemn sin—in any form—either because it is culturally acceptable or not addressed by the church

If you are inclined to use social media (Facebook, Twitter, etc.), there are innumerable posts expressing various opinions relating to contemporary cultural issues. The list is long; however, a few "hot topics" have made the circuit in the past few months/years. Please know that I land squarely on the scripturally conservative side of this discussion. However, be that as it may, I have always wondered why any Spirit-filled believer would desire to debate whether questionable activities of the unregenerate world are acceptable for Christ followers. This goes beyond the argument of the specific details of Scripture. It does not even approach reasonableness to assume that every cultural change of each succeeding generation would be detailed in the Word of God. God is way too smart for that! Minimally, this bespeaks self-justification; perhaps it travels to the far extreme of explaining to/ for God what is currently acceptable. The Almighty can (and does) speak for Himself. *"Who is able to advise the Spirit of the Lord? Who knows enough to give him advice or teach him? Has the Lord ever needed anyone's advice? Does he need instruction about what is good? Did someone teach him what is right or show him the path of justice?"* (Isaiah 40:13–14, NLT).

- Inspired scriptural truth—relevant for all generations and cultures—is written in unchanging principles.

- The work of the Holy Spirit is to provide the application to the matters that are not specifically named in Scripture.

If/when this happens, the door is wide open to redact any part that does not fit a personal philosophy or even theology. Could the Word of God be any clearer? *"Above all, you must understand that no prophecy of Scripture came about by the prophet's own interpretation of things. For prophecy never had its origin in the human will, but prophets, though human, spoke from God as they were carried along by the Holy Spirit"* (2 Peter 1:20–21, NIV).

> The gravest danger for the church of any generation or culture is to question or challenge the authority of Scripture.

What should be the position of spiritually mature leaders? That, dear friends, is reality!

REALITY 5. Recognizing that unforgiveness (hatred, resentment, hurt feelings) will destroy the believer's spiritual life

There is actually no room for debate here. Jesus made it extremely clear. *"For if you forgive other people when they sin against you, your heavenly Father will also forgive you. But if you do not forgive others their sins, your Father will not forgive your sins"* (Matthew 6:14–15, NIV, immediately following the Lord's Prayer).

> The higher the level of visibility/influence of a leader, the fewer the options to promote/participate in activities that may create confusion for less mature believers, or unbelievers in general.

Strong language. Often guided by our emotional compass, at times it is difficult to get past the pain of an injustice, rejection, or hurt that caught us blindsided. This is true for all of us. However, unless we are blatantly vindictive, an unforgiving spirit seldom dramatically harms the person for whom it is intended. Most believers carry these feeling privately—hidden deeply within their own spirit. And that is where the poison is released and the damage done. Perhaps it is gradual. The end result is the same. Churches are divided, families separated, businesses lost as a result of such animosity. Only by the grace of God and the gentle work of the Holy Spirit are we able to find release from the bondage of unforgiveness. The reality is that it simply is not possible to live in spiritual health with an unforgiving spirit. The beloved apostle John wrote, *"We love each other because he loved us first. If someone says, 'I love God,' but hates a fellow believer, that person is a liar; for if we don't love people we can see, how can we love God, whom we cannot see? And he has given us this command: Those who love God must also love their fellow believers"* (1 John 4:19–21, NLT, emphasis mine).

Believe me: the medicine is not worse than the cure!

MY THOUGHTS:

LISTENING IN THE SPIRIT

As Pentecostals, we often have extended discussions about praying in the Spirit. Theologians search the original intent and meaning of the Scriptures to properly distinguish between personal prayer in the Spirit and the supernatural manifestation of the Spirit in an assembled body of believers (1 Corinthians 12–14). Words are parsed in attempting to determine whether the use of the phrase prayer language is measurably different than "speaking in tongues as the Spirit gives utterance." All of these are worthy points of discussion.

My one word of caution is that we never assume ownership of the Spirit's ministry in and through us. His presence is sacred and should never become learned behavior. Being a vessel (although imperfect) through which the Holy Spirit flows is never routine. So, be it in personal prayer, prayer for others, or a supernatural manifestation, there should be a reverent awareness that God is at work to accomplish His divine purpose that is far beyond our comprehension.

However, allow me to view this matter of praying in the Spirit from what is possibly a novel perspective. In order to do this, two basic assumptions are required.

1. True communication can exist only if there is a speaker and a listener. To be effective, both parties must (at some point) be engaged as the speaker and the listener.

Communication has often been described as a two-way street. Now, let's apply that to praying in the Spirit. We automatically assume that praying in the Spirit encompasses only our speaking, in a language that we have not learned. Not so. If there is to be genuine dialogue, the Spirit must be given opportunity to speak while we quietly listen to His voice.

2. There is a distinction between being obedient to the Spirit in our daily walk (Galatians 5:16, 24–25), which leads to righteous living, and listening in the Spirit for revelatory insights and divine guidance. In the first, the Word of God is illuminated and applied to our particular spiritual growth process in/by/through the Spirit. The prayer of Jesus clarifies the significance of the Word and the Spirit being linked in the practical expression of faith. *"Sanctify them through thy truth: thy word is truth"* (John 17:17, KJV). A few hours earlier, He had told the disciples, *"When he, the Spirit of truth, is come, he will guide you into all truth"* (16:13, KJV). For the latter, I would refer to the apostle Peter and the direct instruction he was given to go to the house of Cornelius (Acts 10). Remember Peter remained very Jewish in his tradition and practice. Even though he had preached with power on the Day of Pentecost (Acts 2), the prejudice against Gentiles (anyone other than Jewish) had not been totally eradicated. Notice Peter was praying when he saw the vision. By the way, the word trance is used only of Peter's experience (10:10) and Paul's experience in the Temple in Jerusalem (22:17). Paul was also praying when he received divine instruction. This word trance is transliterated as ecstasy in English and also implies amazement and surprise by the revelation.

Regardless of your word preference—from the scriptural "mediation" (a practice the devil has sought to corrupt) or "waiting on the Lord" all the way to the contemporary carpet time (not my personal favorite choice)—the concept is actualized in listening rather than speaking. I fondly recall the altar services that were a common practice after the sermon in Sunday night worship services. Following any special appeal (i.e., salvation, healing, Spirit baptism, etc.), the pastor would give a general altar invitation. All the saints would kneel and wait on the Lord. At times there was a crescendo of praise, but more often than not there was quiet weeping or praying softly in the Spirit. From those moments came powerful testimonies of what the Spirit had specifically said.

Some brief thoughts on how this might become a personal reality...

1. Be alone in the presence of God. I love church and corporate worship. It is both scriptural and uplifting. However, listening in the Spirit is not a group activity. It is a personal, private moment in which the Spirit speaks directly to the individual. Have you ever wondered about the unique relationship David had with God? Perhaps it was because he spent so much time alone with Him. The sheep he tended were an occasional distraction, but it seems quite logical that he had many hours, day after day, to meditate on the good things of Jehovah God.

2. Select a time and location where distractions are virtually eliminated. No iPad. No iPhone. No MP3. No CDs (even worship ones). Just quietness. This is extremely difficult for this generation as they are not accustomed to silence. Also, with the hectic patterns of life, just finding any extra time is challenging. Here we must learn the spiritual significance of prioritizing the activities to which we feel a strong sense of urgency/need. Actually, the truth is, we make time to do the things we really want to do! For some it may be before the household awakens; others may find the most serene hours after the family has retired.

3. Be intentionally disciplined so that this level of communication in the Spirit becomes a behavioral pattern. I hesitate to use the word habit or compare it with the more mundane routines of life and do so only for the sake of illustration. For those who "need" a cup of coffee as the first activity of the day...how do you respond if it is not available? The very least reaction is that you know you are missing something that has become significant to you. The analogy is obvious.

Self discipline is a major component is spiritual development and maturity.

4. Expect the relationship to develop. Being in His presence, listening in the Spirit, does not become boring or lose its luster. Marcia and I have been married almost fifty-seven years. Our relationship is far more intense now than it was half a century ago. We love being together; it is not a burdensome chore that we simply tolerate. We even know what the other is thinking—sometimes it's scary! I have half-jokingly said that we can carry on a conversation from the platform to her place in the congregation without a word being spoken and without anyone else knowing it. Centuries ago, the prophet Isaiah penned it so well: "*They that wait upon the Lord shall renew their strength; they shall mount up with wings as eagles; they shall run, and not be weary; and they shall walk, and not faint*" (Isaiah 40:31, KJV).

5. A submissively obedient response is appropriate. In simple terms, the Holy Spirit will not persistently push Himself on a resistant heart.

> If one believes that the Word is inspired, the Holy Spirit is God, and that He speaks the will of the Father, then there is no validity to an ongoing debate with the Spirit.

Further, it is humbling to be invited to participate in such a place of confidence with the holy God.

This is not some weird form of Christian mysticism or being out of touch with earthly realities. The opposite is true. Being attuned to the Spirit provides insights into the eternal plan of God that are seldom known or understood by human intellect and logic.

And, by the way, the final chapter of Revelation declares, "*And the Spirit and the bride say, Come*" (Revelation 22:17). To which we add our voices with John, "*Even so, come, Lord Jesus!*" (v. 20).

RESOLUTE COURAGE

Courage finds expression in multiple forms; however, in a broad categorization it can be divided into two simple groupings.

1. **Courage of the moment**—spontaneous action or reaction, often without considering the danger or consequences. Many powerful stories of heroism unfold when someone valiantly risks personal safety in a crisis moment. Later he/she is surprised at what he/she did when adrenalin was flowing at maximum speed. Fear was overcome by the extreme urgency of the situation.

2. **Courage for a predetermined outcome**—the long-term, uphill, often self-questioned, disciplined action. Emotional excitement wanes, and public attention moves on to other issues. Now it becomes unrelenting, teeth-gritting determination. Few stay the course, and those who do will quite likely excel in their achievements.

The latter hardly attracts the masses. Some enter the fray only to quickly exit from the arduous challenges along the way. Spiritual life is no different. The Gospel record attests that the disciples had some sterling moments, but when crunch time came—at the Lord's arrest—they all fled

(Mark 14:50). How marvelous is His forgiveness and grace! The subsequent personal infilling of the Spirit indicates their willingness to overcome the failure and move forward again.

Even with relentless attacks of Satan, the bitter rejection of Jewish religious leaders, and misunderstanding of His purpose, Jesus never lost focus of His eternal mission to this earth. He knew the singular reason for becoming the Son of Man and was determined to fulfill the Father's will. Nearing the prophetically announced conclusion of His brief life, every physical test, mental and emotional temptation, and even spiritual distress would overtake Him in one climactic moment. But we must never end our journey viewing this painful picture. He had already announced that the outcome would be glorious. Resurrection was coming shortly! Never doubt for even one moment—our Lord had resolute courage.

Isaiah prophetically declared the Messiah's unwavering determination to complete the earthly mission for humanity's redemption. *"I have set my face like a flint, and I know that I shall not be ashamed"* (Isaiah 50:7, KJV).

As the time for His suffering and substitutionary death approached, Jesus *"_resolutely_ set out for Jerusalem"* (Luke 9:51, NLT, emphasis mine). No doubt the disciples and crowd shouting "Hosanna" envisioned the coming overthrow of the Roman Empire and reestablishment of King David's throne— the much-longed-for restoration of the Jewish kingdom. Jesus knew differently. At this moment in the eternal plan there would be no celebratory banquet. Rejection, pain, and death were but hours ahead. Repeatedly, the Master had spoken of His mission: *"My food is to do the will of Him who sent Me"* (John 4:34, NKJV).

Today, pressures abound. Those who stand courageously for the Savior of the cross have become targets for a demonically inspired culture. A volcano of hell's lava spews accusations against followers of Christ. This should not be surprising or create fear and despair. The two seemingly most prominent spiritual leaders in the early church, Peter and Paul, both intentionally and explicitly addressed the issue of resistance and rejection from unbelievers. But they also spoke inspired words of encouragement. *"Be strong in the Lord and the power of His might"* (Ephesians 6:10, NKJV). The language is actually a strong command. In other words, be courageous and resolute.

- Don't bow under the threat of a fiery furnace. (Daniel 3)
- Don't close the window when you hear the roar of hungry lions. (Daniel 6)
- Don't compromise when you hear the rattling of the executioner's sword. (Mark 6)
- Continue to look to heaven and bless the Lord even when the rocks start flying. (Acts 7)
- "Eighty-six years have I served him, and he has done me no wrong. How can I blaspheme my King and Savior?" The words of Polycarp, a second-century bishop who was told to recant his faith or die. Polycarp was burned at the stake for his unwillingness to deny Christ.[1]

Another great Old Testament example is God's direct word to Joshua. Following the death of Moses, Joshua, who had been Moses' understudy, was thrust into the role of leading a nation who had:

- known only one leader following their miraculous deliverance from Egyptian captivity,
- lived as nomadic shepherds in the wilderness, and
- watched thousands die over a forty-year time span (everyone who was twenty years old or above when they fled Egypt).

As he assessed the challenge of leading a vast multitude of stubborn, faithless nomads, plus the instruction to go into the Promised Land (Canaan) and conquer it for the purpose of settling there to live permanently, apparently Joshua needed a strong measure of reassurance. The Lord told him three times, *"Be strong and (very) courageous!"* (Joshua 1:5–9).

- His word to us is to focus on the eternal promises in the Word.

- Don't be disheartened, distracted, or disillusioned.

- Be resolute! Be courageous!

- Link the two together, and in His timing, victory will follow.

Endnotes

1   *"#103: Polycarp's Martyrdom,"* Christian History Institute, accessed April 30, 2019, https://christianhistoryinstitute.org/study/module/polycarp.

MY THOUGHTS:

SIN IS NOT GENERIC

In a serious group discussion concerning some of the spiritual issues facing pastors/spiritual leaders in the contemporary world, my thinking was tweaked to revisit the important scriptural subject of sin (disobedience to God), especially as it relates to external behavior. For clarification, there is no dichotomy of thought here. As a baseline for understanding, sin is an internal spiritual position of being in a state of rebellion/hostility toward God. Simply, it is unbelief, defined by an unwillingness to acknowledge personal need for salvation through Jesus Christ. However, behavioral patterns are clear external evidence of what is in the "heart of man."

Consequently, this is a significant theme for every generation to examine frequently and through eyes that have been corrected by the lens of the Holy Spirit. The ways of fallen man are juxtaposed against salvation by faith in Jesus Christ and the grace of God that redeems and restores. The descendants of Adam can once again experience the originally intended place of spiritual fellowship with the Father.

There is no doubt that numerous complex theological discussions face the church today, and the comments here are not intended to be an exhaustive list. So allow me to enumerate the two

> There are almost 900 references to the word sin and its derivatives in the Word of God.

or three rather obvious subjects that will quickly surface in almost every conversation on this subject of external behavior (manifestations of scripturally defined evil).

1. How do you respond to homosexuality?

2. What is our stance on same-sex marriage?

3. Is "social drinking" an acceptable practice for pastors/spiritual leaders and believers in general?

Due to contemporary culture and what has been defined as "political correctness," it seems that some have fallen silent intimidated, even refusing to take a biblical position for fear of rejection from culture (even, in some instances, other spiritual leaders). Still others have embraced a level of "tolerance" (as defined by an unregenerate society) that borders on condoning such practices. The men and women who have been chosen by the Almighty to be His spokespersons must not look for alternate interpretations to scriptural truth to avoid criticism or controversy.

In the short term there may be a sense of gratification, but God is never pleased when His moral creation attempts to circumvent His eternal plan.

> The end results of compromising Scriptural Truth will never accomplish the intended purpose.

First of all, the Word of God has not changed. I would caution that we would not alter our hermeneutic on the basis of cultural attitudes/practices. The authority of Scripture is quickly and dangerously diluted if the experience of any generation becomes the measuring rod for sin—or righteous for that matter. These comments are not in favor of being either legalistic or freed from true biblical holiness. As an aside, one needs to have an appropriate definition of legalism—adding a second door to salvation beyond faith in Christ Jesus—before invoking it as a mantra for excusing carnality.

Of course, at this point the discussion intensifies—proper interpretation of the Word. On this, I hope we can all agree. Going forward, the lines become blurred. What was the original intent? What does the original language say? What were the particularities of the generation to whom it was written? On and on. Ironically, even astute scholars disagree on some issues. It is important that we take the entire body of

> The Word of God addresses timeless principles—the Holy Spirit illuminates the particularities!

Scripture ("all Scripture" is inspired) as the basis for our conclusions. From my personal observation, it seems that for some believers a "new revelation" is always exhilarating. Caution: before accepting a previously unknown truth, careful evaluation with/by Scripture is always appropriate. *"Prove all things; hold fast that which is good"* (1 Thessalonians 5:21, KJV).

Most of us have heard, "The Bible doesn't say anything about that..." Humorously said, God is really much smarter than that. The whole of written literature would be insufficient to address every minute detail of each generation's uniqueness. And this brings me to the point of these comments: Spirit-filled/anointed leaders, spokespersons for the living God, have a divine mandate to make application of scriptural truth to contemporary culture. Jesus said the prophets were stoned. Nathan the prophet looked King David in the eye and said, *"You are that man"* (2 Samuel 12:7, NLT). John the Baptist lost his head for not being silent (Matthew 14:3–12). They did not speak in platitudes. Sheep need a shepherd.

Both by words and example, the message should be crystal clear and diamond bright. It is not enough to simply say that sin is wrong. From the principles revealed in God's Word, sin must be identified.

> You cannot lead from the middle!

This is not being harsh. In fact, it's just the opposite. Does a young child know that fire is dangerous? The younger (in the faith) followers of Christ must be shown the way to *"walk in the Spirit"* (Galatians 5:16–25, KJV), *"put off...the old man"*

(Ephesians 4:22–32, KJV), and *"lay aside every weight and the sin that so easily entangles us"* (Hebrews 12:1–3, MEV).

NOW, ABOUT THE ITEMS MENTIONED IN THE INTRODUCTORY COMMENTS:

1. **Homosexuality is sin.** Paul states that it is a perversion of the God-ordained intention for the man-woman relationship (Romans 1). For those who want to explain this evil away, the arguments are often loud and long. But a loving child of God is not bigoted or intolerant by declaring this truth. Certainly, we would conclude that any mention of stealing or lying should be avoided as it would be an affront to those who practice such sin. I believe in a God of mercy and grace—the cross of Christ is the most dramatic picture of a loving Father. But this very same loving God requires His creation to turn away from sin. The message of forgiveness is always coupled with a "go and sin no more" phrase (John 8:1–11). You are on firm biblical ground to preach/teach deliverance from the enemy's strongholds by the power of the Spirit.

2. **There is nothing more basic than the relationship that God established between man and woman at the very time He placed them here on this earth.** Same-sex marriage cannot fulfill that relationship. Two members of the same sex cannot reproduce—as was the instruction given to Adam and Eve (Genesis 1:28). This is much more than a cultural issue. It is spiritual rebellion against the Creator. While those who may engage in homosexual activities may attempt (in some instances) to hide it from public view, the same is not true for same-sex marriage. My deep concern is that young people are being indoctrinated to be tolerant of those who choose this "lifestyle." A friend recently shared with us that his six-year-old grandson told his parents that his first-grade school teacher had said it was OK if his parents were both men or both women. In the homes of believers, in Sunday school (Bible classes), from the pulpit, the evil influence of this world must be confronted.

3. Social drinking has become a most controversial subject among conservative, Bible-believing Christians. Arguments concerning the correct interpretation/meaning of Scripture abound. Before proceeding, let me state emphatically that I do not drink any form of alcoholic beverages. My personal conclusions are based on Scripture. Obviously, words can be parsed. One drink is not being drunk, etc., etc. So the discussion escalates. But let me come through the back door on this. How many lives are ruined by alcohol? Families are decimated. Women and children are abused and neglected. Thousands are killed or injured annually in automobile or workplace accidents. The medical profession links excessive drinking with various illnesses and diseases. Among the first questions a doctor will ask when doing an examination is, "Do you use alcohol?" An honest conclusion is that this is a blight on society. So my question is this: Do we desire to see how close we can live to the world or how much of the world we can put aside to draw closer to Christ? Do we need some intoxicating "stimulant" to find joy and peace or even to relax? What about those who were addicted to alcohol (or some other life-controlling habit) before meeting Christ? Do we now show them by our example that if they can just be moderate there is no harm done? The apostle Paul provides instruction concerning the believer's attitude in being an example to others. He includes himself in the desired response. *"So if what I eat (meat offered to idols) causes another believer to sin, I will never eat meat again as long as I live—for I don't want to cause another believer to stumble"* (1 Corinthians 8:13, NLT, explanation mine).

ALLOW TWO BRIEF CONCLUSIONS:

1. Even if I do not come to the conclusion from Scripture that one should avoid alcohol (beer, wine, whiskey), I should be willing to avoid any activity that could be a reflection on Christ or that could potentially lead me or others along a path that would be highly detrimental to spiritual, moral, and societal life.

2. The higher the level of visibility a leader enjoys, the fewer options he/she will have. While it is certainly true that it is impossible to please everyone, to avoid something that is known to be questionable or confusing seems to be a simple choice and of little significance. This is not being hypocritical. Nothing should ever be considered of greater importance than our love for Christ and the overwhelming desire to impact every person in the sphere of our influence with the life-changing power of His love.

This brief essay by no means explores these issues in detail. As you pray with an open heart, the Holy Spirit who lives within will surely guide your path. Please refrain from any defensive justification. I have a deep concern for His church; attempting to look forward with a long-term view is not a new issue with me. (If you have an opportunity, please review *Faded Glory: The Church in a Cultural Crisis*, a book that I wrote on this subject several years ago.)

Sin is not generic. It must be carefully explained on the basis of Scripture over and over again. The pressure that Satan is exerting today is escalating. Jesus is coming for His church soon—a church that is without spot or blemish.

"Earnestly contend for the faith" (Jude 3, KJV).

MY THOUGHTS:

THE LINGERING PRESENCE OF GOD

I am greatly intrigued by the record in the book of Exodus (34:29–35) in which Moses entered the presence of God on Mount Sinai. When he came away from that experience, there was lingering evidence of the presence of God. In fact, God's glory was so pronounced that Aaron and the children of Israel were afraid to come near to him. So Moses wore a veil while he spoke with the Israelites. In other words, without any hype or personal proclamation of his encounter with the Almighty, there was visible evidence of the glory of God.

By the way, it is interesting that the Scripture notes Moses did *not* wear the veil when he reentered the presence of God (v. 34). A simple conclusion: the glory of God was so much stronger than His residual presence shining on Moses' face that it was unnecessary—and perhaps would have even been an irreverent expression of pride for him to have done so. And another aside, the words of Paul in 2 Corinthians 3 do not imply that Moses was self-centered. The apostle is illustrating that by comparison the glory of the old covenant was dim and faded away in light of the new covenant.

Simple thoughts from the text:

1. Moses was not aware that his face was shining brightly until it was called to his attention by Aaron and the children of Israel.

2. His unusual experience in the holy presence of the Almighty was immediately evident to them.

3. The glory of God separated Moses from those who did not have the same experience, and not understanding what had happened, they became afraid and fearful.

4. The veil Moses wore was not needed when he returned to the presence of God.

Now, take a moment to consider today—over three thousand years since the biblical experience of Moses. We are a TV generation. In the most intense moment in a program, the station breaks for a commercial. What happens to the viewers? Do they talk about another subject? Leave the room? Get something to eat or drink? The point is that the intense emotion is broken. However, as soon as the commercial break is over and the drama of the story returns, the viewers jump right back into their emotional involvement.

What does this have to do with the story of Moses? Let's put this into a worship format, either corporately or privately. Can we bounce in/out of God's presence as easily as we do with a TV program? Unfortunately, at times I think we attempt to do so. Here is a scenario that I have personally witnessed: A strong time of praise and worship occurs—God's holy presence is evident. Then, there is a significant break for everyone to go out in the lobby for coffee, refreshments, and fellowship. After several minutes of laughing/talking/visiting about all sorts of things (from work to athletics), the congregation reassembles in the sanctuary for the ministry of the Word.

Perhaps it is just a personal conclusion, but it seems to me that the holy presence of God is far more sacred than entering/exiting as easily as with any other activity of the day. The fact that an eternally holy God would even allow us into His presence should be the most awesome experience we could ever have. We must never, ever lose the meaning of such a privilege. This is not to imply that our faces will glow (although I have seen many changed countenances after meeting with God), but I do believe that our hearts should be aglow. And what is in our hearts will surely express itself in multiple ways. Others will be able to see/know that we are gloriously changed!

My plea is that we seek...

- to enter His presence more often,

- stay longer,

- leave with hearts/minds captured by His redemptive love,

- His glory shining forth from our lives.

I pray that this day you will have a life-changing encounter with the all-knowing, all-powerful, always present God! He has given you a permanent invitation—through Jesus Christ—to fellowship with Him.

MY THOUGHTS:

Our Dwelling Place

H. MAURICE LEDNICKY
Adapted from Psalm 90

MARCIA LEDNICKY
Arr. by Steve Rose

Lord Thou hast been our dwell - ing place____ in all gen - er - a - tions, For a thou-sand years____ in Thy sight____ are as but yes - ter - day when it is passed; So teach us,_____ teach us to num-ber____ our days that we may ap - ply our hearts to wis - dom; ____ And let the beau - ty of the Lord,__our God be____ up - on__ us.____

THE TRANSCENDENCY OF LEGACY

Much is said in the political arena about "leaving a legacy." And that is not necessarily a bad thing. However, it seems that much of what we hear teeters on the brink of narcissism: "It's all about me. How will history regard my accomplishments?" Often the person himself/herself is leading the parade, flaunting their own greatness. This is not unique or novel to this generation. In fact, both Old and New Testaments provide accounts of those who sought to leave a legacy but did so in the wrong manner.

King Uzziah (2 Chronicles 26) reigned as king in Judah from age sixteen to age sixty-eight—for fifty-two years. What a legacy he was building! He had many outstanding accomplishments; however, *"when he had become powerful, he also became proud"* (2 Chronicles 26:16, NLT). He went into the Temple and personally burned incense on the altar. God had sternly assigned this responsibility exclusively to the priests. When confronted for his sinful act, Uzziah became furious. At that very moment he was stricken with leprosy, banished from the Temple, and lived the remainder of his life in isolation. He ultimately died in shame. The people remembered him by saying, *"He had leprosy"* (v. 23, NLT).

King Herod (Acts 12:20–23) accepted the people's fickle accolades that he was speaking as a god. According

143

to Scripture, King Herod relished their worship rather than giving glory to God. Instantly, he was struck with sickness and was consumed with worms and died. What a legacy!

Jesus, in teaching about greed, told a parable describing a rich man (Luke 12:16–21) who was so caught up in himself that he became the center of his own universe. To dramatically emphasize His point, the Master said the man died that very night. I understand the context of the passage; however, the lesson concerning legacy is also obvious. The parable concludes with a question from the Almighty: "Then who will get everything you worked for?"

For the child of God, our service to the Lord—our legacy—must be transcendent. That is, what we do in His name is far greater than our human abilities, and its purpose extends far beyond our own lifetime. Elijah is a favorite prophet of Old Testament writ. He is the "prophet of fire" who challenged Ahab on Mount Carmel (1 Kings 18) and won. Shortly after this major victory for the Lord, the prophet became discouraged. Finally, the Lord directed him to Mount Horeb (1 Kings 19) and spoke to him in a whisper rather than the bombastic windstorm, earthquake, or fire that were indeed previous symbols of His presence. Ultimately, God gave Elijah three things to do (vv. 15–16). However, if you read the Scriptures carefully, you will note that Elijah did only one of these things personally.: Elijah anointed Elisha to be the prophet in his place. However, it was Elisha who anointed Jehu and Hazael to be kings. The point? The legacy of Elijah was carried forward by Elisha. It did not begin and end with one prophet! As an aside, Elijah and Elisha were complete opposites in personality. My conclusion is that Elijah would not have personally selected Elisha, but it was God's plan, not his. It is as simple as both Elijah and Elisha were godly servants and useful in divine purpose and timing.

The apostle Paul clearly declared that his legacy was for the church to move forward. The final letter to his *"son in the faith,"* Timothy, outlines this (2 Timothy). Space limitations do not allow detailed comments, so here I will simply note some verses from Paul's letters. Paul encourages Timothy (possibly now pastoring at Ephesus) to be strong in his faith and *"teach these truths to other trustworthy people who will be able to pass them along to others"* (2 Timothy 2:1–2). Notice Paul's far-reaching vision: I have taught you; you teach others; they will teach others. There is no hint that the old apostle is attempting to control the future. His singular goal was for the gospel of Christ to be preached. He emphasizes the truth that Timothy has been *"taught"* (3:10, 14–15, NLT). We read, study, and preach the Spirit-inspired words that Paul penned almost two thousand years ago. In them, there is not one hint that he thinks himself to be the most important among his colleagues. In fact, in true humility he declares himself to be the *"least"* among his contemporaries (1 Corinthians 15:9; Ephesians 3:8; 1 Timothy 1:15). What a legacy!

Having been an ordained minister with the Assemblies of God now for more than fifty-five years, I have often wondered why the people in local congregations have such little grasp of the incredible history of this Fellowship. Obviously, this has not been a priority, and seldom do second, third, and fourth generations seek out such information. Add to this the number of people who have little or no church background who have come to know Christ as Lord and Savior over the past half century or so. But I think there is another significant factor. The early leaders of this Fellowship did not wish to promote individuals, but only to promote the person of Jesus Christ as revealed by the Holy Spirit. Any

> Personally choosing a successor of our liking or seeking to make certain that the future follows the particular pattern we established allows little room for the work of the Holy Spirit.

bent toward self-aggrandizement was viewed as pride. I understand this. After I entered the ministry, my parents were extremely cautious about offering any praise to their own son. It would have been an expression of pride. Those early believers took the ever lurking danger of pride very seriously. Perhaps they went to an extreme. Perhaps we need to shift back more in that direction today!

Do we want to leave a legacy? Of course. However, it is not what we have established or built that is ultimately significant.

Others' approval is not the benchmark for our legacy.

While we all sincerely appreciate the kind words and recognition extended to us from our brothers/sisters, that must always be subordinated. All praise/honor must be intentionally and exclusively directed to the One who alone is worthy to receive such glory.

It is what the Lord has done in and through us for His own glory that matters. That's the singular legacy of laudable worth and eternal duration!

MY THOUGHTS:

GOD'S TIMING AND GOD'S WILL ARE INEXTRICABLY LINKED TOGETHER

Recently I had an informal conversation with a choice young man of God (almost everyone fits into the category of "younger" men these days). We discussed a number of things, but the one that prompted this thought process relates to knowing the will of God in finding/fulfilling the place of ministerial service for a given season in our lives. My conclusion:

The directive will of God is always coupled with God's sovereign timing.

This is easily recognized in Scripture. For those who have been privileged to study/learn Greek, you will recall that there are two significant words in the New Testament relating to "times" and "seasons":

- Chronos—denotes a space of time, implying duration, whether short or long

- Kairos—speaks of a season marked by specific characteristics and events

In a general sense, *chronos* expresses the duration of time, while *kairos* indicates that a given time period is marked by certain features. A quick look at one verse of Scripture will clarify this distinction.

> The heavenly Father is not in the back room looking for plan B because plan A just failed.

"*And he* (Jesus) *said unto them, It is not for you to know the times* (chronos) *or the seasons* (kairos), *which the Father hath put in his own power.*" (Acts 1:7, KJV, emphasis and explanations mine)

Jesus is explaining to His disciples that both the length of the period and the events that are specific to that era belong to the Father Himself. In other words, the purposes of the Eternal Father are exclusively under His authority, and it is futile for humans to attempt any modifications. But for our discussion, the obvious takeaway is that God's will and God's timing are inseparable.

You may also want to reference 1 Thessalonians 5:1 and Galatians 4:4. Both of these passages reaffirm that the plan of God is not accidental or determined by last-minute crisis decisions. These "times and seasons" are nonnegotiable. They are permanently etched in sovereign immutability and declared in prophetic inspiration of the Word. He knew from the beginning.

Of course, we all agree that the Sovereign God has originated/ordained the unique plan for man's redemption and restoration to fellowship with Him. But does the same hold true of His will for each of us as individuals? I suggest that it does. Some things require no discussion.

AS FOLLOWERS OF JESUS, WE ARE TO WALK IN HIS FOOTSTEPS.

> "*I am the light of the world. Whoever follows me will never walk in darkness, but will have the light of life*" (Jesus, in John 8:12, NIV).

> "*Whoever wants to be my disciple must deny themselves and take up their cross and follow me,*" (Jesus, in Mark 8:34, NIV).

AS SPIRIT-FILLED BELIEVERS, WE ARE COMMISSIONED TO UNASHAMEDLY BE HIS WITNESSES.

"But you will receive power when the Holy Spirit comes upon you. And you will be my witnesses, telling people about me everywhere—in Jerusalem, throughout Judea, in Samaria, and to the ends of the earth" (Final recorded words of Jesus prior to His ascension, Acts 1:8, NLT).

AS MEMBERS OF HIS BODY (CHURCH), WE ARE ALSO CALLED TO DEVELOP CARING, LOVING HORIZONTAL RELATIONSHIPS.

But God has put the body together, giving greater honor to the parts that lacked it, so that there should be no division in the body, but that its parts should have equal concern for each other...Now you are the body of Christ, and each one of you is a part of it (1 Corinthians 12:24–25, 27, NIV).

These foundational precepts are His will for every child of God, without exception. These lifelong, unchanging responsibilities are clearly expressed and repeatedly emphasized in His Word.

As these truths are general in scope, we now come to the most personal of issues: "What about me? How does 'timing' integrate with my being in the place (not necessarily geographical) God has chosen for me?" Again, I emphasize the significance of each individual finding and following the unique plan that He has ordained for him/her. It must be a priority that is intentionally and vigorously pursued.

If I rush ahead of God's timing—even to do what He has confirmed in my heart to be His divine purpose—it can be disastrous. Consider Abraham (and Sarah) who decided to help God fulfill the promise of a "seed" that would multiply and bless the entire world (Genesis 16:1–6). Every opportunity, as perfect as it may seem, is not necessarily the right step forward. Joseph was not Egypt's prime minister simply because he had God-inspired dreams (Genesis 37:5–11). David did not become the king of Israel the day after being anointed by the prophet Samuel (1 Samuel 16; 2 Samuel 5). Many scholars believe that it was approximately fifteen years from the time David was anointed by Samuel until he actually became king of all Israel.

If I lag behind God's timing, the door of opportunity may slam shut. Fear and timidity are horrible taskmasters. Being tentative can be paralyzing. Emotions of feeling unqualified for the assignment are (should be) normal. By personal testimony a significant number of Old Testament prophets spoke of trepidation about stepping forth onto a public platform. The simple fact is that we are truly qualified for spiritual leadership only by/through the work of the Holy Spirit. Living a life of regret, looking back, wondering "what if" will sap true joy and destroy peace. Faith and the resultant actions are inseparable companions in fulfilling our heavenly vision (Acts 9:1–19; 26:12–19) with earthly obedience.

> Where you are today is as important as where you will be twenty years from now!

Over the years, I have been asked on countless occasions, "How can I properly discern the next step in God's plan?" Please indulge a personal approach to finding/following the faith walk, especially as it relates to those major course-changing ministry decisions. Some men and women of God have been directed by the Lord to alter direction in a supernatural manner. Praise the Lord for such divine guidance! However, I have found that on more occasions than not, the combination of "His will—His timing" has been a process requiring deep self-evaluation and honest introspection.

1. **Wait for the opportunity to find you.** (You don't have to kick the door open!) Being faithful where you are (without resentment, self-pity, or discontent) is God's qualifying process. Be settled in your own heart.

2. **Initially pray about going forward to the next step.** If

there is no check in your spirit, proceed to further investigation. If you cannot find peace in your praying, immediately determine that this specific ministry is not in the plan of God for your life.

3. Carefully review all the available information. Look below the surface. Mistakes are often made by having only a casual overview of the ministry. Know both the expectations of the ministry and your own expectations. Match the two with your gifts. More times than a few, a discouraged youth pastor has confided in me. He accepted the position on the premise that the pastor wanted a "vibrant, growing youth group," so he immediately began an aggressive outreach to the unchurched of the community. Soon, the pastor explained that the primary focus of his vision was the growth and discipleship of the spiritually immature young people already attending the church. Both are important aspects of ministry; however, this misunderstanding may have been avoided if more specific information had been outlined when the process was in the initial discussion stage.

4. Pray again, asking the Spirit to illuminate all the details in the light of His unique purpose for your life. If there is still no check in your spirit, continue.

5. Seek counsel from a trusted, mature spiritual leader. Be certain that this leader will be objective and not just tell you what he/she thinks you want to hear. A godly mentor is more concerned about the long-term outcomes than the excitement of the moment. The missionary ministry of Paul and Silas was confirmed by mature elders through fasting and prayer (Acts 13:1–3).

6. Pray again. Now it is time to make a decision. IF you cannot find peace in your spirit—immediately stop any further consideration! IF you have peace, make an affirmative decision.

7. Go forward! Do not second-guess your decision. Trust God to qualify you for this ministry. There will surely be challenges and perhaps a steep learning curve—but God is greater!

One final observation: difficulties are not a signal that you are outside the will of God. The battle is spiritual. The whole issue of suffering for Christ's sake is not textbook theory. It is very real and cannot be sidestepped. Satanic forces are highly pleased when a true servant of the Lord walks away from his/her God-given place of service because of the pressures that collectively accumulate against him/her. Keep your heart and motives pure, your determination unflinching.

Someday (if the Lord tarries His coming), you will be able to look back over the path He chose and you followed with genuine joy. The Father will receive praise, glory, and honor.

Just wait patiently for his timing!

> *For everything there is a season, a time for every activity under heaven* (Ecclesiastes 3:1, nlt).

MY THOUGHTS:

WHAT I DON'T KNOW ABOUT THE FUTURE—EVERYTHING!

I have lived long enough to hear many "declarations" about the future from well-meaning preachers—for example, some have said Hitler was the Antichrist (great man of peace, looking to make a peace treaty with Israel?). Various numbers have been calculated to arrive at 666 for certain names, assuring that the person is the coming man of sin, etc. Voices have declared with absolute certainty that the Lord would come on a very specific day. Please know that this is not lampooning the eternal truth of Scripture. There are many prophetic insights provided in the Word from which we can establish positive markers to show us the end game. We do know the ultimate outcome, just not every event/personality in the process.

By the way, I do believe that Scripture teaches a pre-tribulation rapture of the church and the Second Coming (Revelation) coupled with a literal one-thousand-year reign of Christ on this earth.

However, it is impossible for man to intellectually reason the minute details of *how* and *when* God will advance and ultimately consummate the time-related portion of His eternal plan. And that relates to each of us individually, as well as to the global timeline. This in itself reinforces the urgency of maintaining an unshakable faith and confident trust in the sovereign wisdom of the Father.

So, while I cannot see beyond this moment or anticipate the next twist in the geopolitical drama or what some political personality will do on the local, national, or global stage or even the next event of my own earthly journey...

I do know—

1. That God is still God!

2. That He is never surprised by human choices— either good or bad.

3. That no governmental system or political personality will ever override His eternally ordained plan.

4. That His perfect justice is the immovable dividing line between mercy and judgment.

5. That every indicator taken from Scripture, human history, contemporary world entanglements, and the free fall into perversion of this generation all shout loudly that our Lord's return is imminent.

6. That I must live according to the plan He has uniquely ordained for my life, with a pure, holy heart before the Father and a godly, righteous character before those in my sphere of personal influence.

Actually, I guess I can identify a few major bullet points of the nonnegotiable future events described in God's Word.

During my childhood years, my parents had a rather large plaque hanging in a prominent place on the living room wall. Its message still resonates in my heart to this day.

My pronouncements for the future are limited, with minimum attention-getting drama, and can easily be passed

"Jesus is coming... perhaps today!"

over as "heard-that-all-my-life" rhetoric. At any rate, I want to be on record as saying it just one more time.

1. Love Jesus above all else!
2. Anticipate His return at any moment.
3. Hold loosely both the earthly joys and frustrations.
4. The time of separation is concluding.
5. Soon the Savior will call the redeemed home.
6. Eternity will radiate His glorious presence.

Be filled with assurance, peace, joy, and hope!

Therefore we do not become discouraged [spiritless, disappointed, or afraid]. Though our outer self is [progressively] wasting away, yet our inner self is being [progressively] renewed day by day. For our momentary, light distress [this passing trouble] is producing for us an eternal weight of glory [a fullness] beyond all measure [surpassing all comparisons, a transcendent splendor and an endless blessedness]! So we look not at the things which are seen, but at the things which are unseen; for the things which are visible are temporal [just brief and fleeting], but the things which are invisible are everlasting and imperishable (2 Corinthians 4:17–18, AMPC).

MY THOUGHTS:

TWO FREQUENTLY OVERLOOKED BIBLICAL PRINCIPLES: REVERENCE AND MODESTY

Cultural attitudinal and behavioral patterns have made some deep inroads into the practices and teaching of the church in this generation. With the New Testament church, it was exactly the opposite. The preaching of the apostle Paul was pointed and gave no quarter for attitudes and actions that were in direct conflict with the purpose of the Cross. Jesus Christ came to redeem mankind from their sinful nature and separation from fellowship with the Father. But God is a holy God, and even though we are saved by grace—through no merit or works of our own—there is much scriptural evidence to convince us that *while grace is free, it is not cheap.* In short, because of our love for Christ and His substitutionary sacrifice, we strive to be like Him in every aspect of life. That requires discipline and resisting Satan's temptations to conform to any cultural philosophy that comes against the purpose of God for His children. This is not bondage; it is the ultimate in freedom. Every plan of God is for our benefit. He is not a cruel despot who delights in making us miserable. As we obey His Word, there is peace, joy, and fulfillment.

Specifically speaking, in recent years there has been a serious departure from two very significant principles of

Scripture. The first, reverence, is so obvious in the Word of God that it hardly even seems necessary to revisit it.

> Reverence for God and His house of worship should be a basic tenet for every believer.

He is the only true Sovereign, deserving of all respect and honor. While I want to address the issue of reverence in the place of worship, it should be noted that God is to be reverenced at all times, regardless of the location or activity.

Please understand that this is not a plea to promote one style of worship above another. It is, however, a call to examine the attitude in which one approaches the Almighty. The house of God (though just a building) has been dedicated for the purpose of prayer, praise, worship, and scriptural exposition. The common thread that brings believers together is the relationship/fellowship/communion with the Father through Jesus Christ. This is always very sacred.

While there is little scriptural insight concerning New Testament places of worship, other than the Jewish synagogues, the Old Testament provides a very detailed description of the Temple that King David planned and King Solomon constructed. It must have been magnificent! Beyond its exquisite decorations and furnishings (1 Kings 5–6), it was considered a very sacred place. *"When the priests came out of the Holy Place, a thick cloud filled the Temple of the Lord. The priests could not continue their service because of the cloud, <u>for the glorious presence of the Lord filled the Temple</u>"* (1 Kings 8:10–11, NLT, emphasis mine). Jesus Himself was highly displeased (showed righteous anger) at the commercialization of this sacred place that was to be used exclusively for spiritual purposes. *"'My house shall be called a house of prayer,' but you make it a den of robbers"* (Matthew 21:13, ESV; quoting from Isaiah 56:7; Jeremiah 7:11).

Understanding that we are no longer under the covenant of ceremonies and feasts does not seem to justify behavior in God's house that is closely akin to an informal time of relaxation.

God is indeed my friend, but I am not His equal! The issue for me is one of attitude. Can one flit in and out of God's presence on a whim? Whenever or wherever we meet with God—corporately or personally—is this not the most significant moment ever afforded to a redeemed soul? He gave His only Son to bear my guilt. Can this ever be taken for granted? The highest order of angelic beings surround the throne of God, singing, "*Holy, holy, holy*" (Isaiah 6:3).

Grace, of course. Joy beyond description. Peace that cannot be overstated. But all these spiritual blessings are enjoyed within the circle of reverence for the loving heavenly Father. Instill this truth in the hearts/minds of children and young people. The God of eternity is not a convenient "go-to guy" when there are insurmountable difficulties. He alone is worthy to be worshiped (reverenced). The very next time you step into His presence, do so with solemn reverence. "*Our Father which art in heaven, Hallowed* (holy, sacred, revered) *be thy name*" (Matthew 6:9, KJV, explanation mine).

The second biblical truth that has somehow escaped many believers today is modesty. This is perhaps more difficult to specifically define from the Scripture, and none of those charged with the responsibility of preaching the Word desire to be ineffective in ministering to this generation. Cultures do change. But where does the principle of modesty supersede the world's flair for attention and acceptance? What do the world's celebrities look like? In many cases, if nothing else comes into play, their behavioral patterns are blatantly contrary to the Word of God. Sexual sins of all kinds, as defined in Scripture, are rampant today. They do not need to be revisited here; we are all too well aware of the statistics. Provocative clothing is surely one part of the equation, but only one part. Often with parental consent (or worse, encouragement), young people are pushed toward activities that should be reserved for the privacy of the married life. As a pastor I recall preaching on the subject of modesty for the child of God. Later, a married lady with teenage children came to my office crying. She said her husband insisted that she dress in a certain type clothing—and wanted her to wear clothes that were even more "sexy." He was a faithful church member.

> The line from modest to immodest is crossed when any type of clothing or activity is intentionally designed to attract attention to one's physical person in a sensually appealing manner.

Closely linked with the principle of modesty is the very clear biblical description of personal purity. For years I have pondered how it is possible for a born-again, Spirit-filled believer to not be nudged by the Holy Spirit in knowing the distinction between what honors God and what craves the acceptance and approval of a very immoral world. To ignore or attempt to explain away sinful behavior in the name of fads and trends—or worse, to justify it—is offensive to the holiness of the Almighty. Of course, the matter of consistent scriptural teaching and personal example are vital.

By the way, this prophetic word is not just for the younger generation. Statistics reveal an alarming number of professing believers—both men and women—who are addicted to sexually explicit materials. It seems apparent that the words of Jesus are applicable here: "*Anyone who even looks at a woman* (or man) *with lust has already committed adultery...in his* (or her) *heart*" (Matthew 5:28, NLT, additions mine). Deliverance is needed! God's power can break this stronghold.

Forgive me if this may be offensive to some; however, I am personally concerned that these two areas are grave hindrances to a genuine spirit of revival in our Lord's church. Until there is serious, honest introspection as we listen to the Spirit's voice, our influence among unbelievers will be very, very limited. Jesus called us to follow Him. Our Lord did not ever say or even imply that the world would cheer us on for our dedication or godly behavior. In fact, He taught the very opposite.

Are we nearing the return of our Lord for His bride? I certainly do believe His coming is very, very soon. Then time is of the essence. This is not a day for "fun and games" as believers. In view of the lateness of this hour, "*let us also lay aside every weight and the sin that so easily entangles us, and let us run with endurance the race that is set before us*" (Hebrews 12:1, MEV, emphasis mine). "*But I say, walk habitually in the [Holy] Spirit [seek Him and be responsive to His guidance], and then you will certainly not carry out the desire of the sinful nature [which responds impulsively without regard for God and His precepts]*" (Galatians 5:16, AMPC).

Would you pause for a few moments in His presence and allow the spotlight of the Spirit to shine brightly into the most recessed part of your spirit? And if the Holy Spirit illuminates any area that has not been cleansed by the blood of Jesus Christ, this is the moment to ask for forgiveness and receive grace.

> "*As obedient children do not conduct yourselves according to the former lusts in your ignorance. But as He who has called you is holy, so be holy in all your conduct, because it is written, 'Be holy, for I am holy'*" (1 Peter 1:14–16, MEV, from Leviticus 11:44; 19:2; 20:7).

MY THOUGHTS:

TEN UNANTICIPATED CONSEQUENCES OF ADAM/EVE'S DISOBEDIENCE

Satan's distortion of the single prohibition that God required of Adam/Eve in the majestic Garden of Eden (Genesis 2:8–9, 16–17; 3:1–3) implied that this lovely fruit would add a new positive dimension to their lives. He convinced them it was being withheld only because God didn't really have their best interest in mind. We tend to be critical of Adam/Eve's gullibility, but remember that Satan is the master deceiver. And without doubt he used "smooth" language. *"You won't die!...God knows that your eyes will be opened as soon as you eat it, and you will be like God, knowing both good and evil"* (Genesis 3:4–5, NLT).

Prior to this, one third of heaven's angels had made the same mistake of listening to his persuasive rhetoric (Revelation 12:3–4). Though cast down from his lofty position in the spirit world, the evil one's goal has never been altered, diminished or abated (Isaiah 14:12; Luke 10:18). His devious scheme was to overthrow God. The man and woman were perfect targets. Satan took full advantage of their innocence, coupled with the God-given power of choice. He proposed an impossible package of promises. *"The woman was convinced. She saw that (1) the tree was beautiful and (2) its fruit looked delicious, and (3) she wanted the wisdom it would give her"* (Genesis 3:6, NLT, emphasis mine).

Surely, our forefathers had no concept of the consequences for their behavior and the spiritual and physical havoc that would follow this one act of disobedience.

The apostle Paul expressed it clearly: *"Everyone dies because we all belong to Adam"* (1 Corinthians 15:22, NLT; see also Romans 5:12).

Before proceeding with this painful thought, we must shout above the noise of sinful behavior that the Creator God is merciful and filled with abundant grace. In and through the suffering and sacrifice of God's only Son, Jesus Christ, is a pathway back into the fellowship the Father made available to Adam/Eve. Though we have personally sinned, there is mercy and forgiveness in the atoning provision of the Cross (Romans 6:23; Ephesians 1:4–7; 2:4–10). This is the all-powerful truth! We must never forget it.

However, the horrific consequence of sin upon individuals and mankind in general must never be understated... It is not just a schoolboy prank to be winked at. It is heaven or hell serious. God means what He says! Unless there is genuine repentance, and claiming God's provision of gracious forgiveness, the ultimate consequence is eternal separation and punishment. With that backdrop, consider the scriptural account of the unanticipated consequences that now dominated and dictated the future of Adam/Eve.

1. Corrupted intellect/awareness of evil (Genesis 3:7)

2. Sense of personal guilt/shame (3:7)

3. Accountability for actions (3:8–11; 4:3–15)

4. Spiritual separation from God/broken relationship/fellowship (3:22–23)

5. Daily survival under difficult work circumstances (3:17–19; 5:29)

6. Reduced intellectual capabilities (1:26, 28; 2:19–20; 3:17–19)

7. Painful childbirth (3:16)

8. Descendants born in depravity (4:4–8; 6:5–7)

9. Physical suffering/deterioration (6:3)

10. Ultimately physical death (Genesis 5; Hebrews 9:27; Romans 8:18–23)

Adam/Eve died *spiritually* the very day of their disobedience. A holy God cannot tolerate evil. Fellowship with the Father has its foundation in purity and holiness. All of their descendants lost that personal right of fellowship with the heavenly Father and for all their best efforts (works) could never earn the right of relationship. How brightly does the master plan of divine grace come into focus! Jesus (and Jesus alone) provided entrance back into fellowship through His sacrificial, substitutionary suffering and death. He paid our sin debt!

Personally, I fear that we often overlook the significance of the other tree that was "in the midst" of the Garden of Eden: the tree of life (Genesis 2:9). There was no prohibition against eating from the fruit of this tree. In other words, if Adam/Eve had not disobeyed, they would have had the privilege of life without physical or spiritual death. But they did sin, and they immediately died spiritually and ultimately also died physically.

Now, again, back to the Almighty's master plan of the ages. The resurrection of Christ signifies man's full and complete redemption,which includes spirit, soul, and body!

God allowed man the privilege of choice. He did not want slaves who were forced to obey and worship Him. He willingly offered full access into His fellowship. Man made a very wrong decision, but a merciful, gracious, loving God refused to abandon or destroy His

> Our spirits have been redeemed—*past* at salvation.
>
> Our minds are being redeemed—*present* sanctification.
>
> Our bodies will be redeemed—*future* through resurrection.

creation. Now, through Jesus Christ, a personal relationship with the loving Father is once again possible. Praise His all-glorious name!

As for those unanticipated consequences? Bad? Indeed! But for the child of God, they will soon be past. Reason to rejoice? Indeed!

Our Lord lives within us now, and soon we shall live with Him!

MY THOUGHTS:

AT THE POINT OF STRENGTH...

I t is often said that Satan will attack us at our *point of weakness*. I certainly would not dispute that, for he will always attack where there is vulnerability. However, I have come to believe that just as often, perhaps more so, the devil will come against us at the *point of our strength*. Immediately following Jesus' baptism by John in the Jordan River and the affirmation of the Father and Holy Spirit, Jesus was led by the Spirit into the wilderness. From my perspective it was at the moment of His baptism, symbolizing death, burial, and resurrection, that our Savior *fully* comprehended His earthly mission. He knew what was ahead! So significant was this dramatic event that Jesus fasted and prayed for forty days and nights. Logically, it would appear that Jesus had this fully under control. Yet the devil threw his full arsenal against Christ immediately following His spiritual reinforcement in God's presence. Satan tempted Jesus at every level (Matthew 4:1–11):

HIS POWER   Authority over creation

Turn stones into bread

HIS PREEMINENCE   Authority over the spirit world

Angels will protect you

HIS PURPOSE   Authority over human depravity

*I (Satan) will give you the kingdoms
of this world*

The ultimate intention of Satan was to achieve what he had always desired to do: overthrow the one true God.

By the way, if our Lord could not have sinned, there would have been no temptation. Temptation requires a choice between options. And, further, if He had no free will, Jesus would not have been fully human like us. *"For we do not have a High Priest who is unable to sympathize and understand our <u>weaknesses</u> and <u>temptations</u>, but One who has been tempted* [knowing exactly *<u>how it feels to be human</u>*] *in every respect as we are, yet without* [<u>committing any</u>] *sin"* (Hebrews 4:15, AMPC, emphasis mine). The book of Hebrews was written to Jewish believers, hence the comparison between the High Priest and Jesus, who is shown to be better than the old covenant.

Let me clarify. In any area of perceived weakness, as sincere followers of Christ, we guard ourselves carefully. We are keenly aware that if we relax for even one nanosecond, the ever-opportunistic enemy, like a skilled boxer, will take full advantage of the opening. *"When the devil had finished tempting Jesus, he left Him <u>until the next opportunity came</u>"* (Luke 4:13, NLT, emphasis mine).

On the other side, we are confident in our strengths. Have you ever heard anyone say, "I would never do anything like that!"? *"Therefore let the one who thinks he stands firm* [immune to temptation, being overconfident and self-righteous], *take care that he does not fall* [into sin and condemnation]*"* (1 Corinthians 10:12, AMPC, emphasis mine). Only by the grace of God are we able to overcome the attacks of the evil one. The truth is that once we declare ourselves to be "strong" in some aspect of the Christian life, the temptation is to rely on self. We may erroneously conclude that our past experiences of victory assure us of repeated future victories in that arena.

Please allow a personal illustration. A few years ago, I penned a book called *The DNA of Faith: Balancing Your Faith with God's Sovereignty*. It was indeed the expression of my own heart after many years of considering the subject of how/where our faith and God's sovereignty intersect and are consistent with the Word of God. Along the way I came to the conclusion that most of the challenges to our faith occur when the circumstance we encounter is beyond explanation or control. Issues that deal with the sovereignty of God in our individual realities force us to carefully examine the depth of our faith. In other words, faith must be objective (in God) rather than subjective (in the result). Of course, the proper course of action is to willingly submit to His wise authority and confidently trust Him—even when we do not understand or sincere intercessory prayer does not produce the desired outcome.

Here is the application about being challenged at our points of strength. First, there is no hesitancy or wavering about where I am on this issue. I am unshaken in faith that God has the power to change any circumstance and that we must call upon His name "in faith believing" for any/all events that occur in our lives. He has all power, beyond any human circumstance or vicious attack by Satan and his minions. But when supernatural intervention is not immediate, my prayers seem to fall back as if they have come against an impenetrable wall. At this moment I must find His grace to be peacefully content in the sovereignty of God, knowing that He will do what is right and best for me—always!

Prior to moving to Bangkok, Thailand, for ministry at the international church (ICA) in early 2006, I had spent a total of two days in the hospital in my entire life (other than when I was born). Now, in the past ten years...

- Four throat surgeries: bowed vocal cords that required implants
- Quadruple bypass heart surgery

- Prostate cancer

- Hip replacement surgery

- Back surgery

And a few other "minor" things like cataract surgery, a hospital stay for a misdiagnosis, etc.

(No pity party here—no plea for sympathy! I am doing wonderfully well in the strength of the Lord.)

All of that to say, this combination of surprise events (to me, not to God) demanded a total shift in ministry focus that I had not anticipated. Initially, with what appeared to be incessant attacks/tests/challenges, it left me wondering what was happening. For the first time in half a century, there was no next step. The path (from a totally human perspective) had abruptly ended. The privilege of being chosen as one of the Lord's spokespersons never ceased to overwhelm me! To say this was not an emotionally difficult moment would be rather disingenuous.

> We see only the *what* of our circumstance.
>
> God knows the *why* of that circumstance!

These were undeniable realities that demanded absolute confidence in God's loving guidance in our lives. So while to this day I still cannot wrap my mind around the *why* of these events, I want to positively declare that God is faithful, and He deserves to be trusted! Oh, and by the way, this all-wise God has been so loving and has continually opened doors of ministry that I could never have anticipated a decade ago.

So when you feel your breath being taken away as you watch a nerve-racking drama unfold before your eyes and what has long been a strong, secure position in your faith be challenged with a frontal attack, just remember you don't have to depend on your own strength.

Can I say it this way? The same God who graciously provides victory over temptation in areas of weakness will also provide victory in the tests that come to challenge the areas of strength.

"So do not throw away this confident trust in the Lord. Remember the great reward it brings you! Patient endurance is what you need now, so that you will continue to do God's will. Then you will receive all that he has promised" (Hebrews 10:35–36, NLT).

MY THOUGHTS:

INTIMIDATED FROM INSIDE

In a brief review of the various missions paradigms from the apostolic era until today, it quickly became obvious that the major shifts in emphasis came from within the church. The apostolic period was punctuated by two dynamic factors:

1. Believers would carry the message of Christ's death and resurrection for man's redemption to the very ends of the earth after the outpouring of the Holy Spirit, complimented by the words of Christ (Acts 1:8).

2. Coupled with the command of Christ was the promise of Christ, confirmed by angels, that He was going away but would return for them (John 14:1–3; Acts 1:9–11). The urgency to complete the mission He had given them was focused on an abiding assurance that the "blessed hope" could be a reality on any given day. It is not ancillary to note that extended periods of persecution, both from the Jewish religious leaders and the Roman Empire, were almost daily events in their selfless sacrifice of spreading the gospel message across the then-known world.

However, when Christianity became culturally acceptable, the persecution stopped. And from that point forward for several centuries, evangelistic zeal significantly diminished. Rather surprisingly, the challenges were not exclusively from governmental authorities but often from changes within the church itself. This is not intended as a lesson in early church history. Consequently, in general terms, from the medieval period (circa AD 475–1450) until the outpouring of the Holy Spirit at the beginning of the twentieth century, the church struggled with periods of internal confusion about the very specific commission of Christ to proclaim redemption/forgiveness/restoration through His substitutionary sacrifice on the cross. Simply, the church short-circuited its God-given mission.

Now, the point of this missive is to say that after a bit more than one hundred years of the current Pentecostal outpouring—which has greatly impacted the entire world—there are unfortunate signs that could produce a chilling impact on world evangelism in this end-time generation. In fact, the three major things are identical to those that negatively impacted the church at the end of the apostolic era.

1. **A diminishing emphasis on the supernatural work of the Holy Spirit.** There seems to be confusion, even among those identified as Pentecostals, concerning the baptism in the Holy Spirit according to Acts 2:4. Supernatural manifestations of the Spirit (1 Corinthians 12) are at times disallowed in corporate worship services or have been relegated to a place other than in the sanctuary.

2. **Be it cultural acceptance, material prosperity, or lack of preaching on the subject, often a less-than-excited expectation for the coming of the Lord is evidenced among many who profess Christ.** If this powerful motivation is not in the picture, it becomes much easier to be content with this present world. From the Scripture and history as well, anticipation for the Lord's return has been one of the compelling reasons for urgency in evangelism, both personal and organized.

3. **Once the two factors mentioned above come into the church, the call for separation from world-likeness (scripturally called holiness) begins to wane and lose its place of importance for the believer.** It is a vicious cycle. Without a consuming desire to serve, please, and follow the example

of Christ, the level of commitment to His Word and His will becomes less and less a pattern of daily life.

While cultural pressures arise from many quarters today, in the history of the New Testament church, any type of external persecution has never been a long-term deterrent to proclaiming the message of salvation in Christ. In fact, the opposite is true. From the apostolic period through every century and even today, many believers have sacrificed their lives for the testimony of Christ. Subsequently, the gospel message has spread even more. Unfortunately, the major culprit for deterring evangelism comes from within the Body. Is the same true in the twenty-first century?

Years ago—more than sixty to be exact—I was the youth speaker for an outdoor family camp. The services were conducted in an open-air tabernacle with a galvanized metal roof. One night while I was preaching, some youngsters began to throw rocks on the roof. You can imagine the noise it made. After the service an elder statesman in the faith came by to encourage me. I will never forget his counsel. He said, "In my lifetime, as the Pentecostal message was first coming into many communities, people would throw eggs and tomatoes at us and even burn down the brush arbors that we had built for the meetings. But in your lifetime, the enemies to the gospel will not be outside throwing rocks; rather, they will come into the church and sit down on the pew." He prophetically enumerated some of the very things we are experiencing today.

We must never be intimidated by voices from without or within! Jesus, in His final dissertation before the Cross, warned against being "deceived" (Matthew 24–25). I tend to think that the primary meaning here relates to internal deception. Remember, He was speaking to His closest disciples and had just rebuked the religious leaders for their hypocrisy (Matthew 23). These Jewish leaders had a powerful influence on the religious community. Following the ascension of Christ, both Peter and Paul had strong warnings for those who would pervert the gospel of Christ.

My daily prayer is that we *listen to the inspired Word of God* and embrace its precepts.

My earnest plea is that we *listen to the voice of the Holy Spirit* as He applies scriptural principles to the events of daily life and warns of dangerous pitfalls and impending dangers in the path.

My great desire is that we *consistently walk in harmonious relationship with Christ* as our predominant focus in every aspect of life.

When it comes to an unconditional surrender to our Master, it matters not what negative advice others may give or the reproach they heap on us. We must never be sidetracked from *"serving [our] own generation by the will of God"* (as Paul spoke of David in Acts 13:36).

- The majority of the more than seven billion people alive today have not yet come to a full revelation of Jesus Christ.

- The power of the Holy Spirit will enable us to penetrate the blackness of spiritual darkness in every segment of society.

- Jesus is coming very, very soon.

- There is not even one day to delay our sincere intentions to follow the unique purpose He has designed for each of us!

Father, help me to stand strong in faith and never waver!

"POUR CONTEMPT ON ALL MY PRIDE"

During the music portion of the worship at a recent Missionary Renewal service (gathering of Assemblies of God missionaries from all across the globe), we sang the old, old hymn (written by Isaac Watts in 1707) "When I Survey the Wondrous Cross." It has a powerful message of personal devotion emanating from a dramatic realization of the meaning of the cross of Christ.

As I viewed the lyrics on the screen, one line seized a tight grip on my heart: *"Pour contempt on all my pride."*

The dangers of pride are well known. Lucifer (Satan) was cast down from his lofty position in heaven because of pride. He deceived Adam and Eve in the garden by appealing to their pride. The Scripture is filled with tragedies resulting from pride. King Saul, Nebuchadnezzar, Herod—just a few whose lives were decimated by yielding to the evils of pride. Satan's temptation of Christ was laced in a scriptural context (Matthew 4) but was surely an attempt to lead the man Jesus to succumb to pride, just as Satan himself had done in eternity past.

Perhaps the most often repeated verse on this subject was penned by the wise man Solomon. *"Pride goes before destruction, and a haughty spirit before a fall"* (Proverbs 16:18, MEV).

The unveiled truth is that we all struggle with pride. It is a constant enemy, lurking in the shadows of our minds. And it does not necessarily follow that it is always identified by some rather dramatic, overt, self-aggrandizing action. Perhaps more likely is that pride is far below the surface of the visible, securely obscured from the attention and scrutiny of others and, perhaps at times, even ourselves.

So, as we sang, my mind strayed from the other lyrics in this great hymn (I know that this is unique to me and has never happened to anyone else!) to areas that potentially could infect our spirits with this dread disease.

RELEVANCE—Being "out of touch" with present reality is always distressing.

Teens often accuse their parents of not knowing what is happening in their world. Politicians are voted out of office because they are not aware of the needs/desires of their constituents. But there is a very thin line here for the believer. Being culturally relevant can be valuable only to a certain point. If any dilution or compromise of scriptural principles is the by-product of relevancy, then it should be abandoned. Adopting a standard of behavior because "everyone" is doing so seldom (if ever) beams a signal of righteous behavior. To willfully forge ahead, overriding our own character, allowing integrity to slip from our grasp in proving that we are relevant, can be identified only as the consequence of pride. Man's approval is fickle and fleeting. Look at the trends of the day—tomorrow they are history. Something else is new, and the crowd is gleefully chasing after the latest fad. Brothers, sisters, we must never, ever diminish the message of the cross of Christ. Just for the record: the simple gospel of salvation by faith in Jesus Christ is always relevant!"*Pour contempt on all my pride.*"

RECOGNITION—All the sacrifices of service, time, and finances we have given surely deserve some form of recognition.

And, realistically, it is a bitter pill when others who have done little or nothing are applauded for their good works. Even worse is when another receives credit for your ideas or service. Then there is the matter of falling into the trap of spiritual elitism. Look at who I am. My biblical knowledge, maturity, or experience places me at a level high above others in my sphere of influence. Of course, we all know the instructions of the Lord. He used strong language against the Jewish religious leaders whose motivation for their actions was to *"be seen of men"* (Matthew 23:5, KJV). The *"well done, you good and faithful servant"* (Matthew 25:21, 23, MEV) is the only recognition that really matters. The Greek word Jesus used is "bond servant," indicating the servant is totally bound to his/her master. By the time of Christ, this word for servant/slave meant that the commitment was either voluntary or involuntary. In the scriptural context, speaking of the "servants" of the Master, it is always expressed with dignity and respect for the individual.

However, knowing objectively and acting subjectively are often poles apart. To grow resentful toward others or be filled with self-pity is rooted in pride. To view others as though our righteousness has elevated us to a special place of favor with God is without doubt an insidious form of pride. Each day we must refocus on the One we are following and the purpose of our service for Him. *"Pour contempt on all my pride."*

REPUTATION—NOW THAT'S A GOOD THING.

The Bible confirms it. *"Choose a good reputation over great riches; being held in high esteem is better than silver or gold"* (Proverbs 22:1, NLT). The New Testament further clarifies this concept. Spiritual leaders should have a good reputation both with people in the church as well as those who are not believers (1 Timothy 3:1–7). So where does the potential for pride creep into the picture? Simply, it's when one's reputation becomes a matter of supreme importance. Bending the truth here or there, giving it a little "spin" that makes you look good. Being a "name-dropper." Just at the right moment telling a story (even though it may be totally accurate) that will draw attention to what others think of you. Oh, it is subtle indeed. But eventually it can become a huge thorn in the spiritual heart. A healthy dose of personal and spiritual honesty, guided by a godly desire to walk in integrity, is the best antidote for such private pride. "*Pour contempt on all my pride.*"

Perhaps you can join me in honestly offering this prayer...

Oh, mighty God, we are totally unworthy of Your love and grace. In humility we now bow before You. Save us from our sin and ourselves. May we always focus on the price of our redemption and never in pride on what we may assume to have become outside Your grace. It is only in Your love that we experience peace and forgiveness.

Lord, before You, I now pour contempt on all my pride.

MY THOUGHTS:

SINGING ON THE WAY TO WORSHIP!

An interesting collection of Psalms—fifteen of them to be exact—that are known as the *Songs Of Ascent* provide a very succinct approach to worship. And, by the way, these were psalms/songs that were sung *on the way* to worship. Scholars have offered several possible/plausible explanations for the frame of reference in which the Jewish people would sing these songs recorded in Psalms 120–134.

1. They were initially sung as a collection by the exiles who were returning from Babylonian captivity during the time of Ezra/Nehemiah. (Psalm 126 would seem to substantiate this conclusion.)

2. Others have concluded that Jewish pilgrims would sing them as they came to celebrate the three major festivals (Passover, Pentecost, Tabernacles) each year in Jerusalem.

3. Another lesser-known thought is that the Levites sang these specific psalms as they ascended into the Temple courtyard.

Recently I set about to locate one or two verses in each of these psalms that encapsulated the overall message (as it spoke to me). It seemed that meditating on each of the songs—they are all rather brief—might stimulate our personal devotion and worship. (For the preachers/teachers/group leaders, this could be a great series.) So, without commentary, let me list a verse or verses from each Song of Ascent.

(All quotations here are taken from the New Living Translation)

PSALM 120:1—"*I took my troubles to the Lord; I cried out to him, and he answered my prayer.*"

121:5, 8—"*The Lord himself watches over you!... The Lord keeps watch over you as you come and go.*"

122:1—"*I was glad when they said to me, 'Let us go to the house of the Lord.'*"

123:2—"*We keep looking to the Lord our God for his mercy.*"

124:1–2—"*What if the Lord had not been on our side? Let all Israel repeat: What if the Lord had not been on our side...?*" (My personal favorite!)

125:4—"*O Lord, do good to those who are good, whose hearts are in tune with you.*"

126:5–6—"*Those who plant in tears will harvest with shouts of joy. They weep as they go to plant their seed, but they sing as they return with the harvest.*" (What great insight into the struggles and rewards for the faithful servant of the Lord.)

127:1—"*Unless the Lord builds a house, the work of the builders is wasted.*"

128:1—"*How joyful are those who fear the Lord— all who follow his ways!*"

129:4 — *"But the Lord is good; he has cut me free from the ropes of the ungodly."*

130:3–5 — *"Lord, if you kept a record of our sins, who, O Lord, could ever survive? But you offer forgiveness.... I am counting on the Lord.... I have put my hope in his word."*

131:1–2 — *"I don't concern myself with matters too great or too awesome for me to grasp. Instead, I have calmed and quieted myself."*

132:11, 17 — *"The Lord swore an oath to David with a promise he will never take back: 'I will place one of your descendants on your throne.... Here I will increase the power of David; my anointed one will be a light for my people.'"*

133:1 — *"How wonderful and pleasant it is when brothers live together in harmony!"*

134:2 — *"Lift your hands toward the sanctuary, and praise the Lord."*

AMEN and AMEN!!

Singing all the way to the Lord's house!

MY THOUGHTS:

Faithful is the Lord of Hosts

Lamentations 3:23

H. MAURICE LEDNICKY

MARCIA LEDNICKY
Arr. by Nate Carter

Faith - ful is the Lord of hosts.___ Faith - ful is the Lord of hosts.

His mer - cies are new ev-'ry morn - ing. Faith - ful is the Lord of hosts.

It is of the Lord's mer - cies that we are not con - sumed; Be-cause His

lov - ing com-pas - sions nev - er, nev - er fail. Faith - ful is the Lord of

hosts.___ Faith-ful is the Lord of hosts. ___ Faith-ful is the Lord of hosts.

184

STRATEGIES AGAINST THE CHURCH...

In the Old Testament book of Ezra, there is a very relevant type of the various strategies the enemies of our Lord and His Church are attempting in order to negate the plan of God for this period of grace. Ezra, a Jewish priest, returned to Jerusalem at the end of the Babylonian captivity to reestablish the monotheistic worship of the Jewish people. Remember that the judgment of God came in harsh reality against His chosen people because they had blatantly violated the First Commandment: "*You shall have no other gods before me*" (Exodus 20:3, ESV). Do you recall the words Jesus spoke just after Simon Peter declared Him to be the "*Christ, the Son of the living God*" (Matthew 16:16, ESV)? Jesus responded by saying, "*I will build my church, and the gates of hell shall not prevail against it*" (v. 18, ESV). (This is one of only two times that the word church is mentioned in the New Testament prior to the Day of Pentecost. Jesus used the word both times.) So before we proceed with the example from the Old Testament record, let us be fully confident that Christ Jesus is victorious, and even the "gates of hell"—the strongholds of Satan and his minions—will neither defeat nor destroy His Church!

Now for a brief review of the events in Jerusalem following the seventy-year captivity of the Jewish people in Babylon. For a more detailed account of this time period in Jewish history, one would do well to read both Ezra and Nehemiah. These events actually follow the end of the "kingdom era" for Israel. Not from the time of the Babylonian captivity until today has there been a king ruling Israel. (Of course, the devout Jews continue to look for their Messiah—and He will come!) Just a simple time line of leaders and how the story played out is noted here.

- In 536 BC Zerubbabel returned to Jerusalem with approximately 50,000 exiles to rebuild the Temple.

- In 457 BC Ezra (the priest), with approximately 1,750 men, returned to Jerusalem to purify the Jewish worship/religion.

- In 444 BC Nehemiah returned to rebuild the city wall of Jerusalem. This was accomplished in just fifty-two days!

To be certain, this entire process was not an overnight project. In fact, it was ninety-two years from the time that Zerubbabel arrived until the wall was completed under Nehemiah. That in itself offers a variety of lessons for us to carefully consider. But that is a discussion for another time.

Ezra 4 guides us in being alert to several ways in which enemies of the Cross will attempt to defeat and destroy the church in this grace period for the Gentiles.

INFILTRATE

"The enemies of Judah and Benjamin heard that the exiles were rebuilding a Temple to the Lord...so they approached Zerubbabel and the other leaders and said, 'Let us build with you, for we worship your God just as you do'" (Ezra 4:1–2, NLT).

How easily is this observed today! Consider a few of the more glaring attempts of the "enemies of the cross" to deceive (infiltrate) the church:

- The Word of God is not the final authority, as it contains errors and is not relevant for modern society. Pick and choose the parts you accept, and discard the remainder. In short, each person can define his/her own truth/reality.

- Repenting of sin and receiving Jesus Christ by faith is not the only way to eternal life. The cry for unity among all religious persuasions has been embraced from many pulpits. The depravity of humanity is dissed, and the word sin is whispered only among the faithful—and that in hushed tones.

- Acceptance of deviant lifestyles (homosexuality, lesbianism, same-sex marriages) is no longer seen as perversion but, at best, is ignored or, even worse, is propagated under the guise of not offending unbelievers or championed as the latest evangelism technique.

> The message is still the same: Jesus Christ came to forgive sin. He did not come to embrace sin!

- Such scripturally identified sins as fornication, adultery, greed, materialism, and the like hardly even cause an eyebrow to be raised in many churches. There is an incessant pressure to accept and be tolerant (according to a very unscriptural definition of tolerance) of a culture defining its own brand of spirituality.

The subtle petition is "Let us join you, for we are also God's children."

Lest this point be misunderstood, no one has or will ever achieve absolute perfection on this earth (except for our Lord). The church is the place for those who are seeking to find peace and freedom from guilt in an atmosphere of genuine love and acceptance. However, the church must never compromise a single truth revealed in the Living Word of

God for the sake of accommodation. As redeemed children of God, we are still called to separation from world-likeness. True, the process of spiritual maturation (sanctification) is a lifelong work of grace in all of us. With ears tuned to the voice of the Holy Spirit as the Word is applied to this culture, it is imperative that we be spiritually sensitive and wise, following the good example set by Zerubbabel and the other leaders who refused to allow these enemies to infiltrate the work on the temple.

INTIMIDATE

"Then the local residents tried to discourage and frighten the people of Judah to keep them from their work" (Ezra 4:4, NLT).

One person can protest about any Christian activity (Bible reading, prayer, the posting of the Ten Commandments, nativity scenes, etc., etc.), and believers are made to appear as bigots of the most despicable nature. Because we are believers and do not wish to get into a street brawl or shouting match, the tendency is to be silent and simply back away from confrontation. Of course, it is important that we maintain the proper spiritual decorum in every situation. In other words, angry shouting and vitriolic accusations seldom accomplish anything worthwhile. Generally, the chasm is only widened when such hostile confrontation occurs. However, the Lord's work—including being an exemplary and verbal witness—must not be silenced by those who are constantly demeaning followers of Jesus Christ.

> As the god of this present world, Satan is very resistant to the loss of any of his territory!

There is an old adage: "Throw a rock into a pack of dogs and guess which one will howl." Obviously, the one that is hit. Without being judgmental, it would appear that self-justification is often at the core of such vicious attempts to discourage the testimony and lifestyle of those who walk in faith.

Although the negative comments are often excused as philosophical, tolerant, or a personal belief system, this is indeed a spiritual battle.

Think about this: we are as close to hell as we ever need to be. Jesus declared that at the very "gates of hell" His church would be victorious (Matthew 16:18). So, dear saint, do not tuck your head and timidly shrink away from such accusers. Look straight into their taunting eyes with the peace and joy of the Lord gleaming from your sanctified eyes. You are not powerless—the Holy Spirit lives within and He provides wisdom and strength for every occasion. God's grace is always sufficient, even in the most difficult of times.

DECIMATE

"They bribed agents to work against them and to frustrate their plans" (Ezra 4:5, NLT).

It is impossible to predict what may happen in the coming years. Many evil forces are at work. Already the spirit of anti-Christ has been released like a deadly virus around the world, invading every segment of society. Not only are radical extremists who desire to annihilate Christians and Jews (both of whom represent the purpose of God for man's redemption) constantly terrorizing them, but others in the name of pluralistic justice are also overtly and subversively seeking to eliminate the freedoms of individual and corporate worship. Physical persecution is a dramatic reality in many nations of our world and may well move into other countries that have long since been considered as safe havens for religious freedom. Realistically, it is not a very encouraging scene IF one considers only the visible actions that are spawned by evil hearts.

My purpose is not to elevate feelings of fear/despair about the future. Rather, it is to exalt the supremacy of Jesus Christ. A new level of assurance and confidence in the unfailing promises of the Lord will rise in our hearts. He will build His Church!

Jesus did not say... "I will build your church"
Jesus did not say... "You will build my church."
Jesus did say... "I will build my church."

No matter what Satan and his minions attempt, they will fail.

No matter how effectively the ungodly develop their strategies against the church, they will never succeed.

The church will be neither defeated nor destroyed! It has not only survived but is also thriving in even the most unlikely places of our world.

Hold tenaciously to His hand, listen closely to His voice, and carefully walk in His footsteps.

Be encouraged today—He continues to build His Church!

MY THOUGHTS:

SPEAK WHEN SPOKEN TO!

When I was a youngster (in the last century), parents often communicated the idea either explicitly or implicitly that when adults were visiting, "children were to be seen and not heard" and to "speak when spoken to." This is not a debate forum, and it is not intended to support or discount such a philosophy. As an aside, in observing present-day culture, it does seem that a healthy dose of respectful manners would restore some measure of civility to public and private deportment.

The instruction to "speak when spoken to" was exactly what the sovereign Lord Himself told one of the most prolific priest/prophets of Old Testament times. The first three chapters of Ezekiel provide an amazing picture of the glory of God. As a captive in Babylon, Ezekiel recounts the dramatic manner in which the Lord called him to speak to the rebellious people of Israel. He was to be a *"watchman for Israel"* (Ezekiel 3:16–21, NLT). It was a challenging assignment with dramatic consequences for disobedience. So, one expects that in obedience Ezekiel would immediately begin to solemnly warn these captive Jews of impending judgment unless they genuinely repented and returned to a heart relationship with the Almighty God.

Here is where the story takes an unexpected turn. The Lord tells Ezekiel, *"Go to your house and shut yourself in...And*

I will make your tongue stick to the roof of your mouth so that you will be speechless and unable to rebuke them...But when I give you a message, I will loosen your tongue and let you speak" (vv. 24–27, NLT, emphasis mine). The dominant phrase in the passage is "when I give you a message."It is not *if* but *when,* indicating that God would provide Ezekiel with the right message at the appropriate moment.

At times it seems that the intellectual denial of God's redemptive plan in Christ is almost suffocating. The unrestrained, raucous anger and violence can be frightening. Evil of every description and dimension is found in every stratum of society—from the penthouse to the impoverished. And, yes, we do have a word from the Lord. The Word and the Spirit are not silent in this generation. In fact, God has always communicated the simple plan—repentance leads to restoration—from the days of Adam until this precise moment. Now, the revelation of Christ illuminates the fullness of that message of restored relationship with the Father.

THE TAKEAWAY IS SEPARATED INTO TWO TRACKS: PULPIT AND PUBLIC

For those who have been called by God to a pulpit ministry:

1. **Preach the Word!** The entire Word of God is always pertinent; however, there are periods of time, impacted by culture, complacency, or carnality, when specific truths are especially relevant. I am appalled that the depth of the Word has often been traded for other nondemanding approaches to the believer's walk of faith. The application flows out of Scripture, not the other way around.

Biblical truth is neither generational nor cultural.

Powerful prophetic voices are desperately needed in leading the church to live in anticipation of our Lord's return.

2. **Depend on the Holy Spirit for guidance and anointing.** The man or woman of God should step to the pulpit with a

strong "Thus saith the Lord" as the foundational authority by which he/she speaks. No two congregations are exactly alike. God has a word specifically directed to each local assembly. The anointing is not found on the internet on another preacher's blog!

3. **Refuse to be influenced/intimitated** by the loud voices of those who are unwilling to make a total commitment to Christ. Sin is sin PERIOD! This does not imply arrogant harshness or spiritual elitism. The opposite is true. Humility before God, recognition of personal unworthiness, and a never-ending wonder of His grace afford the servant of the Savior anointed ability to speak without fear or angst.

> The preacher's private spiritual preparation validates public presentation.

For those to whom the Lord has not assigned a preaching/teaching ministry but who consistently encounter the daily challenges imposed by a very sinful pagan culture:

1. **Consistently live by scriptural principles.** It will (more than likely) generate some resistance/hostility from those who walk in darkness. But by so doing, you are establishing a base of spiritual authority for future encounters. Of course, we must also verbally share our faith in Christ without hesitation/reservation. Example/experience cannot be debunked. It gives credence and clarity to what is verbally reinforced.

2. **Seize the moment** when the Spirit opens the door. We frequently use the term divine appointments when such opportunities are unveiled. For any given messenger to effectively "plant" or "water" the seed (1 Corinthians 3:6–9), he/she must be keenly sensitive to what the Spirit is saying/doing at that precise moment. The intensity of human pain is frequently the catalyst for a person's willingness to look outside himself/herself. Now, with the Spirit's guidance, the believer can meaningfully point to the one Source of help that transcends circumstantial difficulties of even the greatest magnitude.

3. Speak to the specific issue of the moment. All sinful behavior cannot be addressed at one time. Use godly wisdom. The guiding principle is to show Christ as the loving friend who desires to heal and restore every aspect of life. A hurt child is not chastised; rather,is comforted. Instruction comes later. Remember, our Lord did not come to condemn but to offer eternal life (John 3:16–18).

4. Repentance will follow revelation. The Holy Spirit is faithful. He will shine the spotlight of conviction into a depraved, guilty heart. An individual cannot be saved until personally recognizing their lostness. As with the prophets of Old Testament days, God's desire is always for restoration. The loving Father does not want to exclude from His fellowship; He created man for the very purpose of being in His presence.

In the spiritual realm, knowing what to say and when to say it is of major significance. If we are misguided, the outcome could be quite devastating to the individual we intend to point to Christ. Thankfully, in this era of divine grace, we have both the inspired Word and indwelling Holy Spirit to provide the answer to those challenges. Perhaps our place in the church will never reach the dramatic level of the prophet Ezekiel, but we do have a message directly from the Lord for the twenty-first century.

We have been spoken to—now it is time to speak!!

MY THOUGHTS:

DO YOU REALLY WANT TO KNOW?

IT'S COMMANDMENT TEN!

As we prepare for bedtime each night, Marcia and I listen to the Scripture being read aloud (marvelous, these free apps). It leads us directly into prayer, and it also helps to cleanse our minds from all the mental gymnastics of the day imposed upon us by social media, real-time news, and life happenings in general.

A few nights ago, the passage was Luke 18, which includes the story of the (so-called) "rich, young ruler." As the narrator was dramatically reading the words of Jesus, something grabbed my attention that I had never considered before (perhaps you have). So I asked for those verses to be played again (vv. 18–25). And, then to be read aloud. I was immediately intrigued with the dialogue between Jesus and this respected leader in the synagogue he attended.

Just a bit of background. The thrust of their conversation centered around the Ten Commandments (Exodus 20). Remember, during the earthly life of Jesus, the Law of Moses was still the God-given guideline for the Jewish people.

For ease of memory and understanding, the Ten Commandments are often divided into two categories.

- The first four are *vertical*. That is, they specifically address the human relationship with God (no other gods, no graven images, not use His name in vain, and keeping the Sabbath holy).

- The other six are *horizontal* in that they speak to human relationships with others.

Now here is what became clearly obvious as I listened to this biblical conversation:

- Jesus did not even mention the first four Commandments.

Apparently, this man was dedicated and sincere in meticulously adhering to these particular tenets of the Law. This seems evident in that the members of the synagogue had selected him to a leadership position. (A synagogue was required to have at least ten men.) However, when queried about the behavioral standard for gaining eternal life, Jesus mentioned five of the six remaining Commandments (do not commit adultery, do not murder, do not steal, do not lie, and honor your parents). The omission was glaringly obvious to the scripturally well-versed young man. *"What do I still lack?"* (Matthew 19:20, NIV). He quickly knew that Christ had not included the final Commandment.

And that was for a very specific reason. This was the one sticking point to his total commitment. Jesus put the spotlight on his obsessive desire for earthly possessions. *Commandment Ten.*

By the way, the same Hebrew word translated "covet" in the Old Testament is translated "desire" almost three times as frequently. For example, it is used in Psalm 19:10: *"More to be desired are they than gold, even much fine gold"* (ESV). So the intent is that any inordinate/misplaced/evil desire is included in this Commandment.

> Any desire—even for legitimate things—that is out of control becomes sinful.

Something else is unique to this Commandment: it is internal and can be shielded from public observation and scrutiny. The other five Commandments that Jesus enumerated were highly visible. If a person were a thief or murderer or adulterer, sooner or later it would be known. But covetousness? Impossible to see if the individual wants it to remain secret. In fact, in addressing the importance of the Law (in bringing us to Christ), Paul illustrates a keen awareness of his own depravity by referencing the Tenth Commandment (Romans 7:7). It is this same apostle who strongly declared that he had very carefully observed the Commandments (Philippians 3:4–6) prior to meeting Christ.

Another observation: This young man and another man Jesus encountered, Zacchaeus (whose record is found a few verses later in Luke 19), were both rich. However, the similarities end there. Zacchaeus, the tax collector, had cheated and extorted money from law-abiding citizens who were helpless against his governmental authority. So, soon after he met Christ, at the top of his list of previous sinful activities needing major change/correction was the manner in which he had procured his wealth. Although Jesus did not address the issue, he immediately wanted to make this wrong right. On the other hand, there is no evidence that the righteous leader was in any way dishonest in obtaining/using his money. Quite likely, he was generous with those less fortunate. As with other religious leaders that Christ condemned, it is likely that his benevolence was for recognition and accolades.

Let's return to the issue of total commitment for Christ followers.

1. Think about this for a moment. Was Jesus really demanding that he live in poverty? Or was He saying, "You must love Me more than you love any of your possessions"? The same could be said for many other areas of life—relationships, habits, recreation (participation and/ or observation)—that control our thinking/behavioral patterns. Such things in and of themselves may not be sinful, but they can be very strong weights that dramatically hinder our spiritual "race" (Hebrews 12:1–2).

It is a more detailed discussion for another occasion; however, there is a scriptural distinction between being generous and compassionate and not providing for the needs of your own family while caring for those who are less prosperous (1 Timothy 5:8). Balance, as taught in the entire Word of God, is always the correct pattern. It is the "love of money" that produces all kinds of evil (1 Timothy 6:10).

As an aside, there are more than two thousand references to money in Scripture, four times more than to prayer or faith! Fifteen percent of all the recorded teaching of Jesus was about money/possessions. Must be an important subject!

Remember, in our present world, money is required to carry on the Lord's work! Wealth is not the issue; how (use) and why (motivation) must be monitored constantly and honestly in light of the Spirit's application of the Word. Never adopt a critical or adversarial attitude toward individuals who have access to financial resources. They are needed to advance the cause of Christ around the world!

2. The level of our commitment cannot be measured by what we are willing to *give up*; rather, it is measured by those things that we are *not* willing to give up.

3. This event also emphasizes the urgency of one-on-one conversations with the Lord.

> Prayer time should include waiting—listening, not just speaking.

The biblical principle of meditation has so often been corrupted by false and pseudo religions that we tend to shy away from the concept. If that word is offensive, choose another name. However, it is in those moments of quiet listening that the Spirit spotlights the uncovered areas of our hearts and reveals (or reminds us) of things that need to be changed.

4. Finally, the young ruler had a choice. He walked away from Jesus. There is no further amplification of the story in Scripture, but at least one option is that he did not follow the Lord's instruction. And if we follow that a bit further, it would have been easy for him to justify himself by recounting all the good things he was doing. On occasion the choice to fully commit may seem beyond our capabilities, unreasonable, or (in our human thinking) unfair. Really, it never is.

What does Commandment Ten speak to you at this precise moment in your life? Only you and the Lord can see and know that. No condemnation is intended by these remarks. I'm just asking that you pause, examine, listen, and obey!

> Self-justification is never a suitable substitute for obedience.

MY THOUGHTS:

THOUGHTS ON LEADERSHIP

According to Paul's letter to the believers in Rome, leadership is a God-given gift. The apostle notes seven specific aspects of gifting from the Lord, including leadership. *"If God has given you leadership ability, take the responsibility seriously"* (Romans 12:8, NLT). Like all other special endowments from the Lord, leadership can be developed incrementally or squandered recklessly. The Father's intention is that it be used for eternal purpose rather than for personal benefit.

- Great leaders in the church do not assume personal entitlement.
- Their motivation is to equip others to find and fulfill God's plan.
- Their goal is to ensure there are no spiritual, generational, or gender gaps in the body of Christ.
- Their desire is that god alone receives all the glory for everything that is accomplished.

There are no vacuums in leadership. Someone— good or bad—will always fill a void.

You cannot delegate authority; you delegate responsibility to act on your behalf.

Enabling without frequent accountability will result in a power struggle.

Integrity demands that the same guidelines be applied to all decisions.

You make decisions with your *heart,* if at all possible. The criterion for such decisions is that the individual and/or group would gain from the decision.

You make decisions with your *head* when to do otherwise would compromise principles and the individual and/or group would be negatively impacted.

There are times when the worth of the whole must be weighed in decision making.

When *exceptions* are made to the normally accepted standard, the leader must be prepared to provide a valid explanation for such exceptions.

Ultimately, everyone is personally accountable for his/her behavior. This includes those in recognized positions of leadership.

Very seldom will an individual who cannot function successfully in one assignment be able to perform successfully if given a lateral transfer.

Leaders are held to a higher standard than those who follow them. The options for leaders diminish proportionately to their level of visibility.

Leaders cannot divulge all information considered in decisions. Consequently, there will always be those who second-guess the reasoning/motivation for the decision.

Leaders envision the *big picture* and do not consider the moment as independent from future consequences.

Leaders value the individual contributions of each member of the team. Those whose assignment is at the foundational level make it possible for the structure to be erected.

Leaders are not condescending but considerate and caring.

Leaders do not suddenly appear out of nowhere. Becoming an effective leader is a developmental process that requires *informational and attitudinal discipleship* over an extended time.

Predictability in maintaining principles is a virtue to be highly sought after by leaders and will be respected by followers.

Leaders, like winning athletes, stay within the *prescribed boundaries* of the playing field for the entire game.

Leaders do not assume they are the best qualified for all decisions, nor do they feel threatened by those who serve with them. They *surround themselves* with others whose expertise contributes a specific component vital to complementing and enhancing the outcome of the entire assignment.

Leaders understand that *respect* and *influence* are earned through character. They are not automatically bestowed through rank or position.

Leaders are learners. They never stop *observing, listening, asking questions, gleaning, pruning*. They are not afraid to be forward thinking and acting, but do not seek change for personal recognition or self-aggrandizement.

Leaders see *failures* as momentary speed bumps on the pathway toward the ultimate goal. They understand that *innovation* is not standardized and will need to be fine-tuned occasionally.

Leaders are *flexible* and do not resist *adjustments* in nonessential matters. Something is to be gained from every experience, whether positive or negative.

Leaders *do not follow every new fad or trend* without considering its impact on their specific assignment and the people they lead. They do not change direction or scuttle primary functions for the sake of appearing to be out front.

Realizing that any place of service transcends the individual and that transition is inevitable, leaders invest in others for the future. For those who serve well, their *influence and legacy* will grow exponentially.

MY THOUGHTS:

TOO SMART TO BELIEVE

I have become increasingly concerned by the growing number of people who reject a faith walk simply because they are "too smart to believe." Human reason and logic trump any semblance of faith. In the basket of untruths and half-truths Satan told Eve was this same prideful conclusion: God doesn't want you to "know" because then you will have the intellectual ability to decide for yourself what is right/wrong. And since that fateful day, man has attempted to determine his own destiny through human logic and reason. What was the tower of Babel (Genesis 11:1–9) all about? Man was trying to ascend into the heavens—the very realm of God. We smile and think how paltry was such an effort. Yet think about it for a moment. Aren't all human attempts to find equality with God and His infinite wisdom simply an exercise in futility? In Paul's words (2 Corinthians 10:4–5, NLT), it is God's mighty weapons that will *"knock down the strongholds of human reasoning"* and *"destroy false arguments"* and *"every proud obstacle."* Coming from the apostle, this is dynamic. He was the intellectual who fought against the revelation of Jesus Christ. Now he declares that this "mystery" has been revealed, not learned by rational argument! The book of Ephesians is powerful in underscoring this glorious truth.

Of course, it is never wise to debate about God's faith plan for man's redemption. An old adage seems appropriate here: "A man convinced against his will is of the same opinion still."

> While faith is not anti-intellectual, true faith comes by divine revelation, not by having the mental capacity to logically connect all the dots.

Here are some questions that might point us in the right direction...

1. **Do you believe the Bible is God's revelation of Himself to His moral creation?** That is, is the Word of God the basis of faith? *"So then faith comes by hearing, and hearing by the word of God"* (Romans 10:17, MEV). In fact, this is the foundational question. Unless the Word is viewed as authoritative, it is difficult (impossible) for any person to experience redemption from sin and restoration to fellowship with God. My deep concern is that even among those who consider themselves to be born-again believers, the Word of God has become somewhat of an intellectual buffet: take what you like and leave what you don't like. Eventually, God is reduced to the level of a human, and He is required to meet the "test" of reason and logic. It will never work!

The Bible states clearly that it is impossible for us *"to understand his decisions and his ways"* (Romans 11:33, NLT).

> God is God, and His ways are beyond our intellect.

Further, at times the Word of God is presented from the perspective of human evaluation and the subsequent conclusions of man's reasoning. For example, debates flourish about the interpretation/application of Scripture in contemporary culture (this is certainly not a statement against proper hermeneutics) until ultimately the spiritual authority of the Word is diminished, if not lost in the battle of the minds. It is certainly true that many new moral questions have surfaced in this generation. But it is equally true that the principles of deliverance and redemption are no less true than they were in the time of Jesus, the early New Testament church, or previous generations.

2. **Do you believe in the miracle of the Virgin Birth?** That is, is Jesus really the Son of God? If human intellect can

explain this away, then the Son of God is not our sinless substitute. We then fall back on human goodness and works to earn our salvation. And that, of course, involves human logic in determining what we must do to earn the favor of God. From Abraham until this very day, the relationship with God is dependent upon a walk of faith, not of works (see Romans 4–6). This is one of the two supernatural events that distinguishes Christianity from all other world religions. While it is not appropriate to worship Mary, we must not lay aside the significance of this glorious event. Jesus was born without the depravity (sin nature) of Adam. He is the "second Adam" who never yielded to temptation. He took the Word of God and His Father's stated will as the defense against all the attacks of Satan (Matthew 4).

3. Do you believe in the miracle of the resurrection? That is, did Christ conquer death, which is the ultimate consequence of human disobedience? While many will recognize Christ as a historical person and even give lip service to the resurrection, it is a challenge for the human intellect to view this miracle as the

> The cross is central to our salvation; the resurrection is the confirmation of our salvation.

linchpin of our salvation. The mind muses, how could a Jewish teacher who was put to death by crucifixion two millennia ago have anything to do with my life? To be honest, the human mind cannot grasp such personal intervention of a loving God. But it is true. Christ is not still on the cross! He is not encased in a glass mausoleum! He is *still* alive today! *"Jesus Christ is the same yesterday, and today, and forever"* (Hebrews 13:8, MEV, emphasis mine). And His life assures each of us that we can have eternal life by accepting in faith the covenant promise (Romans 10:9–10).

4. Do you deny the reality of anything spiritual that cannot be adequately explained by human knowledge, reason, or logic? That is, do you believe in the supernatural intervention of God in the events of life? The human intellect is prone to attach a scientific, medical, or coincidental happening to divine intervention. It seems at times even among believers the first tendency is to search for some logical explanation. Can I say it gently: God does not need our explanations. He is the Sovereign. His power is not limited by finite (time-related) restrictions because His power is unlimited. As one person said, "God knows all things, but sometimes He doesn't tell us." And that is OK!

So, the simple conclusion is this: Don't allow the intellect to become a barrier between you and the Almighty. He is the all-wise God, and in faith you can trust Him completely. Someday we will see clearly, and perhaps He will give us the answers to our questions. However, I rather believe that when we enter His eternal presence, such frivolous thoughts about the why/wherefore/how won't interfere with our worship of the thrice Holy God!

MY THOUGHTS:

WHATEVER HAPPENED TO NUMBER 9?

From the earliest days of the twentieth-century outpouring of the Holy Spirit in the USA (Azusa Street in Los Angeles, California; Topeka, Kansas; Houston, Texas, etc.), this community of faith has been recognized as a "holiness" movement. As a part of the worldwide Pentecostal Fellowship, the Assemblies of God (USA) adopted a Statement of Fundamental Truths in 1916. There have been modifications in wording from time to time, but the foundational truths have remained substantially intact for the past hundred years.

This is not intended as a lesson in developmental history of the Assemblies of God; however, I believe the question being posed is a valid one: Whatever happened to number 9?

In the normal order of listing in the Assemblies of God official document of fundamental truths, sanctification is noted as number 9. So that we are all thinking in the same direction, the following is taken from the Assemblies of God website:

9. Sanctification

Sanctification is an act of separation from that which is evil, and of dedication unto God.
- *Romans 12:1,2*
- *1 Thessalonians 5:23*
- *Hebrews 13:12*

The Scriptures teach a life of "holiness without which no man shall see the Lord."
  • *Hebrews 12:14*

By the power of the Holy Spirit we are able to obey the command: "Be ye holy, for I am holy."
  • *1 Peter 1:15,16*

Sanctification is realized in the believer by recognizing his identification with Christ in His death and resurrection, and by the faith reckoning daily upon the fact of that union, and by offering every faculty continually to the dominion of the Holy Spirit.
  • *Romans 6:1–11*
  • *Romans 6:13*
  • *Romans 8:1,2*
  • *Romans 8:13*
  • *Galatians 2:20*
  • *Philippians 2:12,13*
  • *1 Peter 1:5*

In short form, sanctification is both instantaneous (at the moment of repentance/conversion) and progressive (conforming to the image of Christ in daily living by the inner work of the Holy Spirit). Salvation is the baseline.

Sanctification is the ongoing outflow of relationship. This discussion relates to the progressive, inner work of the Holy Spirit following the new birth in Christ. Any other self-directed effort toward spiritual maturity results in either devastating failure or self-imposed discipline/legalistic duty.

It is little wonder that so many have a negative reaction when the scriptural word *holiness* is used. Perhaps a poor analogy, but it bears the resemblance of a child being given horrible-tasting medicine while being firmly reminded by his/her parents that "this is good for you."

For the sake of clarification, it must be understood that all Christ followers are not at identical levels of spiritual growth/maturity. If you are a more mature believer, it is not being "sanctified" to judge or criticize those who have not yet embraced certain scriptural principles. Ours is to be a credible witness with a recognizable history of obedience. Remember, compassion and love are the first prerequisites of being a godly example/mentor. Christ died for the salvation of every human. He is building His church! Our effort is to bring them to understand redemptive relationship/fellowship, providing both opportunity and reason to turn away from the past and move forward in grace.

As with all aspects of being a disciple/follower of Christ, it is much easier to hear the concept and give credence to the theory than to embrace/actualize the truth. Granted, there are (far too many) illustrations in which various extreme approaches to sanctification have surfaced and even for a while become preaching points. Even so, that in no way diminishes or negates the truth of God's Word.

Sanctification is difficult. It is both objective and subjective. The lines often become blurred, and the tendency is for human nature to remain "un-crucified." Self-justification gradually, conveniently, moves away from the ongoing challenges of abandoning world-like behavior. The subjective aspect of holy living (synonym for sanctification) is a moving target. Literally.

Consequently, this definition of the faith walk is constantly vulnerable to extremes. Juxtapose the immature believer who has a severe case of "carnality" alongside the self-righteous person who has made every attempt to abandon external actions that are less than righteous. Judgment and accusation are far too often the end result.

An honest evaluation of the Spirit's work of sanctification in many believers leads us to a painful conclusion: the tilt in recent years has been decidedly more toward pleasing the flesh than walking in the Spirit. Acceptance of humanistic philosophies and unscriptural cultural mores is becoming increasingly visible in the local church.

From my perspective, we are at a crisis junction. "Going back" to scriptural truth/practice is not regression to an earlier time; it is "moving forward" in the eternal plan of man's redemption.

Has this biblical priority been overlooked, forgotten, or simply abandoned to accommodate the cultural preferences of the twenty-first century? Are we not instructed in the Word to lay aside the elements of this world that can deter, distract, damage, or even destroy our personal relationship with the Redeemer, Christ Jesus?

So what are some elements of spiritual character that need to constantly be evaluated in this earthly journey toward eternal redemption?

1. Focus: "Remember Lot's wife" (Jesus in Luke 17:32, KJV). The account of Lot's deliverance from Sodom, along with his wife and two unmarried daughters, is legendary (also biblically true; Genesis 19). Lot's nameless wife experienced a miraculous deliverance from the judgment of God; however, her focus/affection was on what she was leaving behind, not the favored future God had provided.

Amazingly, the children of Israel complained after being delivered from the horrific bondage of Egypt and wanted to go back (Exodus 14:10–12; Numbers 11:4–6).

> Paul declared, *"I press toward the mark"* (*Philippians 3:14*, KJV).
>
> Paul instructed, *"Set your affection on things above"* (Colossians 3:2, KJV).

Unless and until our singular focus is to live a life that honors and pleases the heavenly Father, our spiritual growth will be thwarted.

2. Sensitivity: *"He that hath an ear, let him hear"* (message to the seven churches of Asia Minor as recorded in Revelation 2–3).

If we know the Scriptures, if we are Spirit-filled, how then can biblical principles that are applied to contemporary culture by the indwelling Spirit simply be ignored?

Spirited worship in the assembled body of believers can be spiritually/emotionally encouraging, and anointed preaching of the Word can be persuasive; however, to simply compartmentalize/relegate that experience to one and a half to two hours per week will never provide spiritual victory/maturity. The argument that "the Bible does not mention…" is totally invalid for the child of God who is intentionally/earnestly listening for divine guidance in the everyday course of life. While it is true that *the Lord looks on the heart,* that poses no comfort to those who are using the passage as a proof text to justify personal carnality.

(As an aside, 1 Samuel 16:7 has nothing to do with justifying certain behavior or style of dress; rather, it refers to physical size. Remember, Saul was "head and shoulders" taller than most Israelites; David was not.)

3. Predictability: One might choose the word conviction (quite different than an opinion) or consistency or discipline. The ever-vacillating emotions/feelings must be subservient to the will. What is often referred to as "situational ethics" is not in the believer's guidebook. Right and wrong are not determined by location, associations, or majority behavior. True sanctification is in process when my will is becoming submissive to HIS will. Pushing the limits toward world-likeness in the name of "spiritual liberty" or "relating to culture" is neither scriptural nor productive. Carnality (thinking/acting like unbelievers) is explicitly defined as a deterrent to spiritual growth.

4. Time: Any discussion of sanctification would be incomplete without a pointed focus on the sanctification of time.

Dare I even mention the enticing grip of social media, if its harm is nothing more than a consumer of valuable time? Comments/directives about prayer and Bible reading are common and often leave the believer with guilt feelings.

So why do these very basic elements of faith pose such challenges? Quite likely the most frequent comments would relate to time. Some are indeed valid. But then in the light of full disclosure, how does the legitimate stack up against the discretionary use of time? Without being judgmental, let me ask you to consider your own personal time. One example is sporting events (attending/watching on TV/reading in the newspaper/etc.). Me? I am a "news junkie," which is really rather useless since the same "news" is repeated every fifteen minutes!

Having said that, failure to read the Word and commune with the Father is symptomatic of a deeper love-relationship problem.

5. Energy: Growing toward spiritual maturity requires our very best efforts. Yes, the Holy Spirit at work within is the "sanctifier." However, according to the Scripture, the believer must be actively involved in the process.

Paul says to *"put off the old man"* and *"put on the new man"* (Ephesians 4:20, 24; Colossians 3:1–15, KJV). The subject of these verses is either explicitly stated or strongly implied as "you." In other words, a part of sanctification demands intentional self-control and personal discipline. It sounds so trite, but God will not force you to live a holy life. It is His plan, but only total commitment today—and everyday—will bring us to new levels of Christlikeness. The high-energy infusion we need is found in the power of the Word. By the Holy Spirit through prayer and humble obedience, spiritual maturity/holiness is actualized in daily living.

We often hear gospel songs about the "valleys" of life and others about the "mountaintop" experiences. The simple truth is that most of life is a journey through the "plains" of daily living. Boring, tedious at times, but surely teaching us the value of living by faith no matter the current circumstance.

> *"Take this whole world, but give me Jesus...I won't turn back..."*
>
> *"To be like Jesus...all I ask—to be like Him..."*
>
> *"Keep me true. Lord Jesus, keep me true...there's a race that I must run..."*

Those choruses (and many others) sung in years past were pungent prayers. The focus was on Christ—away from this present world and toward the eternal home.

As a follower of Christ, never, ever forget number 9!

Jesus is coming soon!

MY THOUGHTS:

OCCUPY TILL I COME

"Occupy till I come…" These words are often quoted from a parable in Luke's Gospel (Luke 19:11–28, KJV) that Jesus told on His way into the city of Jerusalem at the beginning of Passion week. This parable is quite similar but distinct from Matthew's account (Matthew 25:14–30). It is an interesting study to compare the two, but that is for another occasion. Suffice it to say that Christ was emphasizing:

- the urgency of being prepared for the Master's return,

- the understanding that His earthly kingdom would not be established and that moment,

- the utilization of God-given resources to bring Him honor and glory.

(Just a passing thought: this could be a good sermon outline.)

Let's consider three possible responses today to this admonition:

OCCUPY TILL I COME

In my opinion it is impossible to not observe how quickly we are approaching the end of this age. One need not be a scholar in biblical prophecy to see what is happening all around this world. The news media blares out the evidence daily. It is found not only in a few individual nations but also in the global spiritual struggle of heretofore unknown (and even unthinkable) proportions. The Scripture explains it clearly as the law of sowing and reaping: *"For they sow the wind, and they shall reap the whirlwind"* (Hosea 8:7, ESV). From my understanding of Scripture, the events of today are quickly moving into place for the coming Antichrist to be revealed. Be encouraged; God's purposes will be accomplished. The Lord will surely come soon for His church (rapture of the redeemed)! So, as believers, how do we react to the dramatic events of each day?

1. Do nothing. Just go along with our own life interests and preoccupations/occupations, assuming that while the world is changing, it doesn't significantly impact the plans for my personal life. This is not intended as a harsh, judgmental comment. We all have varying levels of responsibility that are significant and must be attended with careful attention. But it would be helpful for us to evaluate the structure of our priorities from time to time. Where on our list of priorities are worship (corporate, family, personal) and witness (home, family, friends, business associates) positioned? A simple question we can all ask ourselves: What dominates my thoughts? What can I always make time in my schedule to do? In light of our Lord's soon coming, we must be engaged in His service. Occupy till I come.

2. Focus on the future to the neglect of the present. Back in 1988, a book entitled *88 Reasons Why the Rapture Will Be in 1988* became very popular in Christian circles. People were selling their possessions and moving into communes to await the Lord's arrival. Families had "rapture parties" to tell their unsaved family members good-bye and divide up their possessions. A genuine belief that the Lord could come for His church in a specified time period grew to such an extreme that it ultimately had a very negative influence on many people, both believers and unbelievers. The skepticism grew exponentially, especially when the rapture did not occur that year. Unfortunately, in many quarters for fear of being classified as an extremist, the message of our Lord's return has been either neglected or omitted. Jesus did indeed tell us to *"look up, and lift up your heads"* (Luke 21:28, KJV) when the evidence of His return becomes more and more apparent, but He has not rescinded His plea to *"look on the fields"* (John 4:35, KJV) that are harvest ready. In light of the Lord's soon coming, we must be engaged now. Occupy till I come.

3. Strengthen our resolve in sacrificial service. I have long believed that the level of our commitment is determined not by what we are willing to give up but rather by what we are not willing to give up. No one can make that determination for another. The older must not assume that their time of effective service for the Master has been completed. The younger must not assume that, at some future date when life (work, children, etc.) is not so demanding, they will find a place of service.

Paul urges the believers at Ephesus to "redeem the time." The Amplified Bible Classic Edition says it very well: *"Look carefully then how you walk! Live purposefully and worthily and accurately, not as the unwise and witless, but as wise (sensible, intelligent people), making the very most of the time [buying up each opportunity], because the days are evil"* (Ephesians 5:15–16, AMPC).

Both lifestyle witness and verbal witness are scripturally mandated. In obedience to the instruction of Jesus, we dare not try to affix dates to our Lord's return. However, in His final words to the disciples prior to His ascension back into heaven, the resurrected Christ told them two important things: (1) The Father alone knows the "times and seasons," and (2) the Holy Spirit will empower you to "be my witnesses" in all the world (Acts 1:7–8). The point of concern was to share the message by the power of the Holy Spirit. This remains His instruction to each of us today. In light of our Lord's soon coming, we must be engaged intentionally. Occupy till I come.

As an aside, some great songs (of another generation to be sure) emphasized the privileged urgency of occupying in His service.

They define the church as embracing the return of Christ as a foundational doctrine. Practically every sermon among earlier Pentecostals included direct reference to being prepared at all times for His coming. One of my favorites is *The Songs of the Reaper*. The words of the chorus are powerful:

We'll work till Jesus comes.

Work, for the night is coming.

> *Over and over, yes, deeper and deeper,*
> *My heart is pieced through with life's sorrowing cry.*
> *But the tears of the sower and songs of the reaper,*
> *Shall mingle together in joy by and by.*

(Taken from Psalm 126:6)

Glorious day when we hear the Master say, "*Well done, good and faithful servant. You have been faithful over a little; I will set you over much. Enter into the joy of your master*" (Matthew 25:23, ESV).

MY THOUGHTS:

THE FOUR MOST SIGNIFICANT SUPERNATURAL MANIFESTATIONS DURING THE "TIMES OF THE GENTILES"

Having recently celebrated Pentecost Sunday, which is commonly called the "birthday of the New Testament church," I began to reflect on the most significant events that relate to this period of God's grace for all mankind. Personally, I believe that four supernatural manifestations of God's person/presence/power/glory mark this period in the eternal provision for man's redemption—from the sinful state of broken fellowship to restored relationship with the Creator.

A few comments that are axiomatic to these conclusions:

- The "times of the Gentiles" (in a broad sense; Luke 21:24) encompass the period from the end of the Jewish kingdom era (Babylonian captivity) until the second coming of Jesus Christ to this earth to reestablish the throne of David (millennial reign).

- A manifestation of God's person/presence indicates that in some way God was personally revealed—either visibly or made known by specific actions through one of man's senses (i.e., speaking in other tongues).

- Each event was prophetically declared by Old Testament prophets, even though these anointed prophets did not fully comprehend the event and/or its ultimate fulfillment.

For those who believe the Word of God is the inspired message from God to man, these foundational truths need little, if any, explanation. However, please suffer just a brief comment regarding each of these supernatural manifestations of the almighty God.

1. THE MIRACLE OF THE VIRGIN BIRTH OF JESUS

From man's fall in the Garden of Eden, the human lineage has been tainted—depraved, with a bent toward sin. The Scripture makes it clear: *"All have sinned and fall short of the glory of God"* (Romans 3:23, NKJV). No exceptions. So every child born to Adam and Eve and those born from that day forward until now through the natural reproductive process do not have the capacity to pay the penalty for their sins. A holy God cannot accept an unholy sacrifice. Only a pure/perfect sacrifice would be acceptable. In the marvelous, incomprehensible plan that God initiated, His Son—known to us as Jesus—was conceived by the Holy Spirit and born to a young virgin (pure, without previous sexual experience). He became one of us but chose not to sin and disobey the Father as the first Adam had done. Now, HE could pay the sin debt for all mankind. No other human could qualify. What an absolutely glorious provision! Of course, we know that for the sacrifice to become effective, Jesus had to die. And die He did, in a brutal, unmerciful manner.

2. THE MIRACLE OF THE RESURRECTION OF CHRIST

It was the resurrection that confirmed the validity of the sacrifice. He defeated the ultimate consequence for man's sin—death. As the "firstfruits" of those who die and are resurrected (1 Corinthians 15:20), Jesus guaranteed our ultimate and total redemption. The very last enemy to be defeated (rendered ineffective) is death (v. 26). But because He is alive, we shall live forever in a glorified body that is like our Lord's (1 John 3:2).

These events were not hype or myth—God revealed himself personally to man! This is part of the progressive, revelatory plan of the all-glorious God.

3. THE MIRACLE OF THE OUTPOURING OF THE HOLY SPIRIT

Also prophetically proclaimed in the Old Testament and verified by annual ceremonial celebration was the outpouring of the Holy Spirit—that was to be "upon all flesh" (not only Jewish, nor any select segment of society; Acts 2:17). The powerful event, accompanied by the believers speaking in languages they had neither studied nor understood, flung open the door for the gospel message to be transported into "all the world" as a witness to the redemption afforded through Jesus Christ (Mark 16:15; Acts 1:8). It is this power made available by the indwelling of the Holy Spirit (third person of the Trinity) that has enabled the New Testament church to reach around the world. This fact in itself is a direct fulfillment of the words of Christ. How completely must we rely on the Holy Spirit in this generation. This is not an optional accessory. It is standard equipment for the spiritual battles the church is encountering today.

4. THE MIRACLE OF THE RAPTURE OF THE CHURCH (YET TO COME)

For more than two millennia, dedicated followers of Christ have been looking and longing for the return of Christ for His bride. The hope of His return thrust those earlier believers into their world with the gospel. Historically, the Pentecostal outpouring that began approximately one hundred years ago was the natural outflow of a renewed awareness of the soon return of Christ, coupled with the need to bring the lost to Jesus before it was too late for them. From the time I was a very young boy, powerful, prophetic preaching has impacted my life. Someone may ask, "Do you still believe He is coming?" To which I would answer an emphatic "Yes!" With the modern technological developments now making it relatively simple for some of those future events to be fulfilled, the picture of His return is coming into clearer and brighter focus. Again, the Son of God will reveal Himself supernaturally. This miraculous event will be for all who have been saved by faith in Christ. The New Testament church, in which all true believers are included, will be gone from this earth. (The Holy Spirit, who is omnipresent, will not be taken out of this world!) According to Scripture, some will accept Christ as Savior after the Rapture (during the brief rule of the Antichrist). However, the Bride of Christ will be in glorified bodies in the presence of the Lord. This unique moment in heaven is called the "Marriage Supper of the Lamb." After this, Christ, along with these redeemed/resurrected saints, will return to establish His earthly reign of a thousand years. This time He will be revealed to the entire world.

Why is all of this important? To be certain, we do not have an unlimited view of the schedule of divinely orchestrated events. But even a casual overview of what we do know from the revealed Word of God provides a very good picture of who we are as His redeemed children and what we can expect in the future. This simple road map— from the Virgin Birth to the rapture of the church—is hard to misinterpret.

Just a special "birthday" reflection: the church is alive today and earnestly praying for His return.

"And the Spirit and the bride say, Come." "Even so, come, Lord Jesus" (Revelation 22:17, 20 KJV).

THE NEGOTIATOR: ABRAHAM WITH THE ALMIGHTY

The story is recorded in Genesis 18. Sodom and Gomorrah were reveling in their last few depraved moments before the terrifying judgment of God consumed them. The Lord Himself (the preincarnate Christ) was examining the situation. Before He unleashed His just punishment for such extreme perversion, the Eternal Sovereign talked personally and privately with Abraham (Genesis 18:16–33), His friend (Isaiah 41:8; James 2:23).

Remember, Abraham did not live in/near Sodom (Genesis 13:18); however, his nephew Lot had chosen this area (vv. 8–13) for personal gain.

Now, when the Lord spoke of the wickedness of Sodom/Gomorrah, it seems evident that Abraham was aware of the total abandon to sin in these cities. Historians cite many unthinkable acts of punishment for women, governmental and financial corruption, as well as the often-discussed (and scripturally documented) sexual perversion. The patriarch immediately began to negotiate on behalf of any righteous people who were living in that area. Hopefully, Abraham suggested, the Lord could find fifty righteous. Or forty-five. The number kept getting smaller—forty, thirty, twenty, or even ten before a Holy God required immediate accountability. Perhaps Abraham was specifically thinking

225

of Lot and his family. Some ancient studies indicate that Lot had two married daughters, making a total of eight in his family. If there were children, it is conceivable that the lowest proposed threshold for saving the cities could be reached. While only speculation, estimates of the regional population range all the way from a few thousand to one hundred or more thousand. As an aside, I wonder how many Bible-believing followers of Christ could be found in any major city or nation of our world today. The very thought of the pervasive evil of this generation should drive us to plead with God for mercy and forgiveness.

If you follow the scriptural record, the story becomes even more sordid. God did, in fact, destroy those cities with fire and brimstone (burning sulfur) (Genesis 19:24). Lot's wife did not want to leave and became a historical marker—of salt (v. 26)! Subsequently, the two unmarried daughters had sexual relations with their father while he was so drunk he did not even realize it (vv. 30–38). It is evident that a very sinful culture had significantly influenced this family toward tolerance/acceptance of humanistic self-gratification. Hardly can one make a strategic decision to knowingly live in a cesspool of evil—for earthly gain—without becoming tainted by the prevailing attitudes and behavior. Self-justification is the first step toward compromise, ultimately resulting in open disregard for scriptural principles and holy living (James 2:13–17; Romans 1:18–32).

But, with that brief synopsis of the situation, let's return to Abraham's negotiation with the Lord. Think about the apparent boldness of a created being speaking so openly with the One who created him!

1. Abraham had a personal relationship with God. It was more than a casual acquaintance! Each spoke confidentially with the other. Abraham was honest with God about his concerns. There is a backstory to this kind of openly honest relationship. We catch a bit of God's thinking: Abraham could be trusted to do what was right and pass godly values on to his descendants (Genesis 18:17–19). From the creation of Adam/Eve, God's intention was to have a relationship with man that was built on mutual love and trust. The first man/woman experienced the personal presence of the Father in the Garden of Eden (Genesis 3:8). Quite a commentary of the nature of God! When sin destroyed that holy relationship, God in His divine foreknowledge was prepared. Now, from that fateful day until the coming of Jesus as Redeemer, the process of revelation was taking place. Only a few Old Testament saints ever moved into that enviable position of such fellowship. How blessed we are today! Jesus, our sin bearer, at the right hand of the heavenly Father, continually makes it possible for us to have direct access to the Father (Hebrews 7:25).

2. Abraham did not demand anything of God. He understood the vast distinction between the Eternal Sovereign and his own finite limitations. He was God's friend, but he did not consider himself God's equal. By the way, Abraham's grandson Jacob adopted a totally different approach to God. He chose to play the "If-Then" game with the Sovereign (Genesis 28:20–22). Jacob had fallen into the self-preservation mode of thinking. He was negotiating for personal benefit.

God is never opposed to honest questions. This is not a lack of faith. (Thomas is a great example of sincere questioning. Personally, I think "doubting" is the wrong adjective to define Thomas.) However, a dangerous line is crossed when the question is laced with angry or bitter accusations. A very high level of human arrogance is displayed when any person erroneously assumes that he/she can dictate a certain course of action/results in a given situation. From years of personal observation, I have long since concluded that it is human nature to desire situational prominence, if not preeminence. Personal rights and entitlements have a stranglehold on this generation.

3. Abraham did not lose faith because the results were not in line with his requests/desires. He did not blame God, accusing Him of not honoring His Word, nor did he blame himself for a lack of faith. Only a few years later, Abraham, without resistance, did not hesitate to obey the Lord's instruction to offer the promised son, Isaac, as a sacrifice (Genesis 22:1–19). Remember, human sacrifices had never been acceptable to God. This moment was an incredible test of Abraham's confidence/trust in the Sovereign God. It is much later in the New Testament book of Hebrews that we learn of the strength of Abraham's faith; he believed that God would raise Isaac from the dead (Hebrews 11:17–19). The outcome of this humanly inexplicable test is also worth noting—not only the fact that Isaac was spared but also that God explained (to His friend) why this challenge of faith had come. It was to determine his obedience, even when it seemed beyond reason or initially impossible to understand divine ways. In simple terms the Lord was saying, "Now I know that you love *me* more than you love the *blessing* (Isaac)!"

A one-time (or even several-time) action/response from the Almighty that does not match our sincere desire/earnest prayer does not mean that He is unloving, unresponsive, unjust, unfair, unwilling, or unable to answer our petition. What it does mean is that He (alone) sees the end from the beginning, knows what is best for each of His children, has an eternal plan that is unique, and longs for us to have absolute confidence in the wisdom of His ways. Through many years of observation and discussion with distressed believers, it appears to me that long-term faith challenges most often revolve around the struggle to maintain a confident trust that God really is God. Of course, in the throes of a very painful experience, we have all emotionally posed the question "why?" But running to Him, rather than away from Him, leads us to a calm assurance that by faith, through grace, our joy will return. It will be possible to sing, "*Weeping may endure for a night, but joy comes in the morning*" (Psalm 30:5, MEV)!

CONCLUSIONS:

Abraham negotiated with God in relation to the eternal destiny of sin-warped minds and bodies. These people in Sodom/Gomorrah desperately needed forgiveness and redemption. Eternal destruction was just a few hours away. Is it not the same today? Jesus is coming soon—who can deny that prophetically we are traveling at supersonic speed toward the end time/judgments of God? And regardless of your personal eschatological perspective, life is moment by moment for all of us.

> We must not delay our fullest intentions to be interceding/witnessing to unsaved family/friends.

Abraham did not attempt to negotiate concerning his own obedience or the fulfillment of God's promised plan for his future blessing. Did Abraham make mistakes? Did he veer off course? Yes, he (like all of us) was not perfect. But underneath those weak human tendencies, he clung tenaciously to his faith. And to this very day, any serious discussion of Abraham includes the descriptive moniker "father of the faithful"!

The Old Testament narratives have pertinent application for every generation/culture, including the twenty-first century. In realistic terminology (not covering mistakes, failure, or sin), the inspired record points directly to New Testament principles, putting, as it were, a recognizable face to an abstract concept.

1. The Great Commission has not been rescinded (Matthew 28:18–20; Mark 16:15–18). The Holy Spirit was given to empower believers to unashamedly proclaim the gospel: Jesus Christ was born of a virgin, lived a sinless life, died a substitutionary death, rose from the grave, ascended into heaven, and sits at the Father's right hand—and by grace through faith, every estranged person can be forgiven and restored to a personal relationship with the Father.

2. Willful and joyful obedience to His Word is the path to living in peaceful assurance of a celebrated entrance into the presence of God—our eternal home!

MY THOUGHTS:

BUY THE TRUTH...

Nestled among the many wisdom sayings of Solomon, he offers this sage advice to the younger generation: *"Buy the truth, and sell it not"* (Proverbs 23:23, KJV). He concludes that this will make your father and mother joyful (vv. 24–25). This word buy means to be in possession of, to procure by purchase with a price. In short, the "truth" is a possession well worth the price it costs to attain it.

I discovered a simple yet profound lesson about "truth" in John's Gospel. Review it summarily, and then when you have a window of time to do so, examine the Scriptures in greater depth.

God the father is truth. *"And this is life eternal, that they might know thee the <u>only true God</u>"* (John 17:3, KJV, emphasis mine). (See also John 7:28–29.)

Jesus is truth. *"Jesus told him (Thomas), 'I am the way, <u>the truth</u>, and the life'"* (John 14:6, KJV, emphasis mine). (See also John 1:8–9, 14.)

The Holy Spirit is truth. *"But when the Comforter is come, whom I will send unto you from the Father, even the <u>Spirit of truth</u>, which proceedeth from the Father, he shall testify of me"* (John 15:26, KJV, emphasis mine). (See also John 14:17; 16:13).

The Word is truth. *"Sanctify them through"* (John 17:17, KJV, emphasis mine).

The Trinity is the ultimate expression of Truth. I often say that all of God is all of God. There is no disparity or conflict in the attributes of Father, Son, and Holy Spirit. As has been stated, the Father, Son, and Spirit are coequal and co-glorious in essence, substance, and power.

In his historic work *Systematic Theology* (1907), A. H. Strong speaks of Truth as it relates to divine perfection:

> *By perfection we mean, not mere quantitative completeness, but qualitative excellence. The attributes involved in perfection are moral attributes.... So God's activity presupposes a principle of intelligence, of affection, of volition, in his inmost being, and the existence of a worthy object for each of these powers of his nature. But in eternity past there is nothing existing outside or apart from God. He must find, and he does find, the sufficient object of intellect, affection, and will, in himself. There is a self-knowing, a self-loving, a self-willing, which constitute his absolute perfection. The consideration of the immanent attributes is, therefore, properly concluded with an account of that truth, love, and holiness, which render God entirely sufficient to himself.*

> *By truth we mean that attribute of the divine nature in virtue of which God's being and God's knowledge eternally conform to each other.[1]*

> *Truth in God is not a merely active attribute of the divine nature. God is truth, not only in the sense that he is the being who truly knows, but also in the sense that he is the truth that is known. The passive precedes the active; truth of being precedes truth of knowing.*

> *All truth among men, whether mathematical, logical, moral, or religious, is to be regarded as having its foundation in this immanent truth of the divine nature and as disclosing facts in the being of God.[2]*

The logical conclusion to such a thought is that the more we know about God, the greater is our understanding of His divine nature and relationship to His own creation.

For some, all of this seems quite immaterial to everyday living. Like, for example, how to measure a triangle on a sphere. You knew how to do it one time in a geometry class but promptly forgot it on the way out of the class. However, let me assure you it is not useless information. When the deepest struggles of life are crashing in all around us and we must have some absolute anchor to which we can cling, the simple yet profound fact that God is Truth can both guide and sustain us through the crisis. The voices yelling that God is not fair, just, or who He says He is can be quite formidable. But *"God is not a man, so he does not lie. He is not human, so he does not change his mind. Has he ever spoken and failed to act? Has he ever promised and not carried it through?"* (Numbers 23:19, NLT).

> God does not just know the truth; He is Truth in its fullest revelation.

"*All your words are true; all your righteous laws are eternal*" (Psalm 119:160, NIV, emphasis mine).

"*Lead me in your truth and teach me, for you are the God of my salvation; for you I wait all the day long*" (Psalm 25:5, ESV, emphasis mine).

It is little wonder that King Solomon urged his generation to *"buy the truth"* and never, ever *sell it.*

Quite likely, time constraints and daily responsibilities will never afford us the solitude enjoyed by a young shepherd named David to meditate frequently on the greatness of Jehovah God. Or perhaps an opportunity to study the depth of biblical languages and ancient cultures will never be available to us. But there are no limitations or restrictions on personal access to the Father's holy presence (through Jesus Christ). How inspiring to have an earthly glimpse into the eternal majesty of our all-glorious God!

Truth? Not for sale!

Endnotes

1   Augustus Hopkins Strong, *Systematic Theology, vol. 1, The Doctrine of God* (Philadelphia: Griffith and Rowland Press, 1907), 260.

2   Strong, Systematic Theology, 261.

MY THOUGHTS:

ELITISM: A SCHISM WITHIN THE CHURCH

Schism is a strong word. It should not be tossed around flippantly. The original intent as it related to the Christian community was a division or breach that was created by something other than a doctrinal issue. However, as time progressed, the meaning was broadened to include any circumstance that brought disunity/separation among believers. There is ample empirical evidence, both scripturally and historically, that numerous conflicts of sizeable proportion existed *within* the early New Testament Church. Even during the earthly life of Christ, the Jewish religious leaders were belligerent and self-righteous. This was a serious issue to the Son of God. While He always commended these leaders for keeping the Law, He unhesitatingly confronted them for making their "traditions" more significant than the Law of Moses (Mark 7:8–9, 13). They were so successful in instilling their attitudes of superiority into the minds of many devout Jews that their elitism was often the catalyst for confusion and division, even after the Day of Pentecost.

Space does not permit a detailed exposition of scriptural illustrations; however, the Apostle Paul spoke frequently of the elitism/division that was a threat to the infant church.

Paul approaches several significant concerns in his first letter to the believers at Corinth. This young, enthusiastic, Spirit-filled assembly seemed to be filled with a number of

235

deep-seated relational conflicts and doctrinal errors. Early on he gives a broad, general introduction to the specifics that follow. *"I appeal to you, dear brothers and sisters, by the authority of our Lord Jesus Christ, to live in harmony with each other. Let there be no divisions in the church. Rather, be of one mind, united in thought and purpose"* (1 Corinthians 1:10, NLT).

1. Division relating to leadership styles (3:1–11),

2. Division during the celebration of Communion (11:17–22)

3. Confusion during public worship (14:26–40).

4. Misunderstanding of spiritual gifts (12:1–11).

5. Misinformation concerning the resurrection (15:1–58).

Yes, these were Spirit-filled believers. Immature, to be certain, but nonetheless Spirit-filled. Speaking in tongues is not the end-all of spiritual growth. In fact, the baptism in the Holy Spirit is a beginning point for the believer to walk in the Spirit.

Likewise, Paul urged the Ephesians to be united in Christ Jesus (Ephesians 4:1–6) and to *"grow up into [Christ] in all things"* (v. 15, KJV).

John speaks often of "loving one another" (1 John 2:7–11). It is a scriptural principle we dare not treat lightly.

In His "pastoral" prayer (John 17), Jesus pleaded with the Father for unity of believers—in every generation—to be the hallmark of their relationship with God Himself.

Unfortunately, because we are all still in the flesh at varying levels along the spiritual path, we don't always use godly wisdom in speaking and/or in our actions. At times a tone of elitism creeps into His Church.

For a few moments let's consider some real-life situations where elitism may develop in the Body of Christ...

1. A "new revelation" that becomes a single-focus rally

point (i.e., extreme positive confession/material prosperity, etc.). has often translated into an attitude of spiritual superiority. More likely than not, any single-focus message will become distorted or eventually modified from its original scriptural intent. Proponents imply superior spiritual knowledge/depth because of their insight on this previously unknown or overlooked revelation.

> An extreme teaching is usually an accepted biblical truth that has been overemphasized due to an underemphasis of that same truth.

2. Pride in accomplishment—success as defined by cultural standards—in skilled communication, in size of congregation, in position/prominence in the community, etc., can determine one's spiritual identity. Recognition and accolades can be devices of Satan to instill pride in an otherwise humble heart. The wise man Solomon penned, "*A person is tested by being praised*" (Proverbs 27:21, NLT). Sadly, the humorous adage "He believes his own press releases" may contain more truth than any of us would care to admit.

3. A changing culture desensitizes believers through repeated rhetoric. The end result is rejection of scriptural truth (i.e., moral attitudes—fornication, adultery, homosexuality, abortion, etc.) and a sense of intellectual enlightenment to espouse modern doctrinal concepts. The argument of human logic is valid only to other humans. With powerful force Paul writes, "*Oh, how great are God's riches and wisdom and knowledge! How impossible it is for us to understand his decisions and his ways!*" (Romans 11:33, NLT).

4. Unresolved conflict involves an "us-them" spirit. In reality, both the "us" and the "them" may have an unscriptural attitude. Insisting on doing it only "my way" fosters a defensive spirit. Unfortunately, elitism is often a two-way street.

5. Rumors (without factual information) and gossip (with correct information) produce damage to the influence of others and loss of respect for them. The individual with the superspiritual demeanor tends to go on a feeding frenzy

when such juicy information is laid before him/her. There is a proper time/venue to discuss the situation and (prayerfully) come to a wise decision/resolution.

6. Preference is mistakenly assumed to be principle. Be careful! We must not allow our personal expressions/style in worship to be viewed as normative. (Obviously, this is in no way addressing the absolute authority of God's Word.) Quite likely, the elders have through decades of trial and error come to prefer a certain style of preaching/music. The younger generation has decided what style they prefer since it is their only experience. Sounds a bit like Corinth, doesn't it?

Frequent preaching/teaching on the biblical imperative of unity in the body of Christ, living in genuine humility before God and fellow followers of Jesus, loving and forgiving those whose actions are spiritually immature should be considered a very high priority as we earnestly pray for a twenty-first-century outpouring of the Holy Spirit. On the Day of Pentecost *"they were all with one accord"* (Acts 2:1, KJV). Through earnest prayer may it be so in every New Testament church. Love, forgiveness, and respect for other brothers and sisters in the community of faith is the correct scriptural pattern.

Lord, reveal any hidden spirit of elitism in our lives that would hinder unity and diminish the work of the Holy Spirit in the family of faith in which we worship/ fellowship. May we never be instruments of confusion and conflict among your people. Teach us to serve You with deep humility, recognizing that we are totally unworthy of the gift of grace that we have received through our heavenly Redeemer's sacrifice.

MY THOUGHTS:

EXTREME TEACHING IS OFTEN AN OVEREXAGGERATION OF SCRIPTURAL TRUTH

As a general rule, extremes in teaching/practice develop as an overexaggeration of an accepted biblical truth. This is often caused by a lack of balanced emphasis on that particular truth. Any emphasis on one particular biblical truth to the exclusion of other biblical truths will inevitably lead to a distortion of that and/or other truths of the scripture.

COMPONENTS OF AN "EXTREME" TEACHING

- It majors on *one* scriptural truth to the exclusion of other important truths.

- It offers a few *proof* text verse from which the teaching is defined rather than finding the principle throughout the entire body of Scripture.

- Normally it is considered a *new revelation* of truth that had not been previously known but has now been revealed for this particular era of time.

- This *new truth* becomes a rally point—that is, those with "mature spiritual understanding" have embraced it. The implication is that if you do not accept this teaching, you are not in the "flow of the Spirit" today.

- It rejects (as less spiritual) anyone who questions the *interpretation* of Scripture upon which this teaching is based.

- There is usually one *chief proponent* of the teaching who becomes the person to whom others look for insight.

- The *disciples* of this teacher tend to carry the teaching further than the original teacher intended, thus compounding the doctrinal errors.

- In some cases, the teaching appeals to *fleshly desires* disguised as spiritual through Scripture as the justification for self-indulgence/gratification.

It is the flesh attempting to cloak itself in holiness!

The ultimate danger to both the leader and the believer:

Manifestations of the Spirit become a
Method of identification that will inevitably lead to
Manipulation of God's people.

MY THOUGHTS:

PRAISE AND WORSHIP

WE PRAISE GOD FOR WHAT HE DOES

Exuberance, excitement, joyful thanksgiving, shouting, rejoicing, glorifying His name

"The Lord is my strength and song, and He has become my salvation. He is my God, and I will praise Him; my father's God, and I will exalt Him" (*Exodus 15:2*, MEV).

"It is good to give thanks to the Lord, and to sing praises unto Your name, O Most High: to declare forth Your lovingkindness in the morning and Your faithfulness in the night" (Psalm 92:1–2, MEV).

WE WORSHIP GOD FOR WHO HE IS

Reverence, humility, solemn respect, sacred obedience, bowing in overwhelming unworthiness

"O come, let us worship and bow down; let us kneel before the Lord, our Maker" (Psalm 95:6, MEV).

"Worship the Lord in the beauty of holiness; tremble before Him, all the earth" (Psalm 96:9, MEV).

Both are essential for believers—they are inextricably joined together.

Genuine praise will ultimately (always) lead into the holy presence of a loving Father.

Praise and worship should be just that!

MY THOUGHTS:

SUFFERING—UNIVERSAL AND UNIQUE

Although not the most inspirational subject for discussion among believers, the biblical significance of suffering leaped out at me recently while teaching a course on the Pauline letters/epistles. Very rarely did he omit the subject in his inspired writings. It is rather obvious that he considered it a significant subject for all believers, no matter their geographical location or religious or ethnic background. More to that in a moment.

First, let's examine what I have identified as *universal suffering*. Simply, it is the ongoing by-product of the curse. The sin of Adam/Eve in the Garden of Eden brought consequences that extend to every descendant of the first Adam (Romans 3–5). Read the Genesis account of the fall (Genesis 3) and follow the path of human history until this very day, and it is evident that no one escapes suffering. So, even as believers we face multiple difficulties in daily life and ultimately physical death. As an aside, the physical body is still under the curse. The resurrection of the body is the final and ultimate step in our full redemption. And not all suffering, physical or otherwise, is due to personal wrongdoing. Jesus explained it this way: *"For He makes His sun rise on the evil and on the good and sends rain on the just and on the unjust"* (Matthew 5:45, MEV). Perhaps the reverse of that is implied. Drought (to follow

243

the Lord's analogy) also comes on the just and unjust. We must not condemn ourselves or blame God if everything in the course of daily life is not in peaceful continuity, as we would desire for it to be. The distinction for His children is that we understand God is sovereign, His way is always perfect, and His Word is always true (Psalm 18:30). Even more significant is the personal promise of eternal life—deliverance from all aspects of the curse—that is made possible by the substitutionary sacrifice of Christ Jesus. All suffering will be over (1 Corinthians 15:26). God will wipe away all tears!

Now, let's transition to the idea of *unique suffering*. This reference specifically relates to followers of Christ and the suffering coming as a direct consequence of serving Him in full obedience. While it can be rather easily overlooked, suffering is a very significant theme of the New Testament and should be carefully considered.

Paul's inspired letters/epistles are filled with details of his own personal suffering for Christ. And this did not come as a surprise to the apostle. Do you recall the Lord's word to Ananias when he was directed to speak to Saul immediately after his conversion? *"For I will show him how must he must suffer for my name's sake"* (Acts 9:16, MEV, emphasis mine). In fact, in defending his apostleship, Paul recounts all the hardships he has endured for preaching the gospel (2 Corinthians 11:22–28). It is a rather extensive list. Of course, he spent his last earthly days in a Roman prison. From that prison he wrote (in his final letter) to Timothy: *"Yes, and all who desire to live a godly life in Christ Jesus will suffer persecution"* (2 Timothy 3:12, MEV, emphasis mine).

Peter, a member of the Lord's "inner circle" (along with James and John), wrote an entire epistle (1 Peter) about suffering—and how it is possible to live in victory even when enduring extreme persecution. *"Beloved, do not be surprised at the fiery ordeal that is taking place among you to test you, as though some strange thing happened to you. But rejoice insofar as you share in Christ's sufferings, so that you may rejoice and be glad also in the revelation of His glory. If you are reproached because of the name of Christ, you are blessed, because the Spirit of glory and of God rests upon you"* (1 Peter 4:12–14, MEV). Many scholars see the "fiery ordeal" as referring to Nero's (Roman emperor, AD 37–68) sadistic act of tying Christians to poles in the palatial gardens and setting them on fire to provide light for his immoral orgies.

Our brothers and sisters in Christ in many nations have experienced governmental hostility and great physical suffering, imprisonment, and violent death for their faith. With increased frequency there are reports of brutal attacks on worshipers. Even in nations (including our own) that espouse religious freedom, there has been a rather dramatic upsurge in verbal abuse and intimidation against those who believe and obey the Word of God.

Should this dramatic escalation of persecution in these last days catch us off guard? Does it mean that we are not living in faith? Is Satan actually winning? Emphatically not! Read the faith chapter (Hebrews 11) and you will discover that not all the heroes of faith were miraculously delivered. *"And others had trial of cruel mockings and scourgings, yea, moreover of bonds and imprisonment: they were stoned, they were sawn asunder, were tempted, were slain with the sword: they wandered about in sheepskins and goatskins; being destitute, afflicted, tormented;... they wandered in deserts, and in mountains, and in dens and caves of the earth. And these all, having obtained a good report through faith..."* (Hebrews 11:36–39 KJV, emphasis mine).

Beginning with the inspired record of Jesus' earthly life in the Gospels throughout the entire New Testament, all of the authors (Matthew, Mark, Luke, John, Paul, Peter, and James), except Jude, specifically address the subject of suffering for the sake of Christ. If the early New Testament church, minus today's methods of communication, travel, and technology, was constantly barraged with frontal attacks, we can surely expect no less in this generation. This is not political; rather, it is intense spiritual warfare.

Let's draw some conclusions:

1. Suffering is part and parcel of every human life under the curse (Romans 8:22–23). It will not cease until the final enemy of death has been destroyed (rendered of no effect) by the Conquering Redeemer.

2. When bad things happen to righteous people, it implies neither a lack of faith nor a harsh heavenly Father lashing out at His own redeemed children. The horrific consequences of sin often result in deep hurt and pain even for the most dedicated servants of the Lord.

3. Such suffering in the course of life must be understood and accepted in the full confidence that God is sovereign and He has all things under control (James 1:2–8).

4. Suffering for Christ's sake should not come as a shock or surprise to us. The Word of God explicitly informs us that Satan seeks to annihilate all that is of God (Ephesians 6:10–17). The forces of hell are relentlessly attempting to defeat/destroy anything and everything that God has ordained. Christ is building His church right at the portal of hell (that is, the present earth until the curse is destroyed).

5. We are privileged to be part of something much bigger than one individual. Candidly, we are not the main attraction. As loyal soldiers of the Cross, we engage the enemy. But we are always victorious in Christ!

So join me in a commitment to more fully trust in the Lord and not engage in self-pity or feel mistreated by suffering—either universal or unique.

"Though our outward man perish, yet the inward man is renewed day by day. For our _light affliction_, which is but _for a moment_, _worketh for_ us a far more exceeding and eternal weight of glory; while we look not at the things which are seen, but at the things which are not seen: for the _things which are seen are temporal_; but the _things which are not seen are eternal_" (2 Corinthians 4:16–18, KJV, emphasis mine).

MY THOUGHTS:

247

OTHER TITLES BY H. MAURICE LEDNICKY

The DNA of Faith:
Balancing Your Faith with God's Sovereignty

Faded Glory:
The Church in a Cultural Crisis

Kingdom Living

Before You Step into the Pulpit

Observations from down the Road

New Testament Outlines
Book by Book

Old Testament Outlines
Book by Book

The Scriptures Applied

FOR ADDITIONAL BOOKS, ORDER FROM:

www.lednickybooks.com

or

Lifestyle Ministries
1322 North Fenchurch Lane
Springfield, Missouri 65802